The opinions expressed in this manuscript are solely the opinions of the author and do not represent the opinions or thoughts of the publisher. The author has represented and warranted full ownership and/or legal right to publish all the materials in this book.

Out of The Darkness Into the Light
A Memoir
All Rights Reserved.
Copyright © 2014 Dawn Dreyfuss
v4.0

Cover Photo © 2014 JupiterImages Corporation. All rights reserved - used with permission.

Biblical Scriptures are from the King James Version, Amplified, New Living, and NIV (New International)

This book may not be reproduced, transmitted, or stored in whole or in part by any means, including graphic, electronic, or mechanical without the express written consent of the publisher except in the case of brief quotations embodied in critical articles and reviews.

ISBN: 978-0-578-13291-4

Zion Publishing

*I dedicate this book to the God who inspired me to write it.
When I didn't know what to say, You spoke though me.
When I didn't feel like going on, You thrust me forward.
Thank you Lord for believing in me, and
giving me the opportunity to be a blessing with my words.*

Acknowledgements

I would like to express my deepest gratitude to the following people:

My friends and family who encouraged me to persevere with my vision to write this book, and see it through to the end.

Nancy Massand, my editor and my friend. Even though I winced when you pruned, it made the fruit all the sweeter. Because of you, I went the extra mile.

Debra Vatalaro, what a truly gifted artist you are. Your art work on my poems brought them to life.

Mike Massand, your spiritual leadership and guidance during this process has meant the world to me.

My husband John, thanks for believing in my vision. Your suggestions, and input help make this book what it is.

Table of Contents

Out of The Darkness Into the Light i

PART I My Childhood/ Before Spiritual Birth 1
    Chapter 1:   My Family 3
    Chapter 2:   Nanny and My Younger Brother Robert 7
    Chapter 3:   Growing Up Broken 9
    Chapter 4:   Abuse/Addiction 14

PART II Meeting Christ/ Spiritual Birth 35
    Chapter 5:   Revelation—God's Call 37
    Chapter 6:   Saying Yes to the Call 46
    Chapter 7:   Developing a Relationship with the Lord 50
    Chapter 8:   Learning the Lessons of Faith 57

PART III Transformation/ Living a New Life 69
    Chapter 9:   Starting Over 71
    Chapter 10: New Opportunities: Growing in Faith 76
    Chapter 11: Embarking on Marriage 82
    Chapter 12: Margaret's Story of Survival In the
                    Concentration Camp in Dachau, Germany ... 90
    Chapter 13: Love and Loss 97
    Chapter 14: New Beginnings 109
    Chapter 15: Restoration—God's Faithfulness 124
    Chapter 16: Living with Purpose 147

PART IV Poetry..155
  Field of Dreams.. 156
  Child of Promise 157
  Promise Keeper 158
  Queen of Hearts.. 159
  Reaching for the Sky 160
  The Sea of Dreams.. 161
  Freedom... 162
  Time and Time Again 163
  Unity 164
  Lion King 165
  The Fire Within 166
  Warfare 167
  A Beacon of Light 168
  My Dad 169
  Valentine's Day Love 170
  The Colors of Love 171
  Shine Bright the Light..................................... 172
  Whispers in the Night..................................... 173
  Tree of Life.. 174
  To My Daughter 175
  Our Secret Place... 176
  Your Loving Eyes.. 177
  Illusions 178
  New Beginnings... 179
  Living Stones 180
  The Fusion of Love 181
  An Easter Prayer for You 182
  Seasons Blessings.. 183
  To My Mother 184

Prayer 185
Contact Page 186

THE HAND OF THE MASTER

Scarred and torn, wretched and bruised,
The Hand of the Master places me on His wheel.
In His mind's eye, He sees a vessel of beauty
and perfection. He has a vision of this earthen
vessel my eyes cannot see.

His loving fingers start to work me over.
I scream out in protest. With deep
compassion, He comforts me with His Words of
promise. His soothing touch is starting to feel
good.
I'm growing accustomed to the times that He
takes me off the shelf and looks me over.
He inspects every line and crevice within me.
Just when I think I look better than the other
pieces
of clay, He puts me in the oven to burn out the
dross.
In my mind's eye, I no longer recognize myself.
What was once marred and broken, has taken on
the shape of a beautiful piece of art.

Cannot the Creator mold a masterpiece more
intriguing and glorious than the sunflowers?
He no longer puts me on the shelf.
My position has changed.
I have become His special project.
I now sit on the altar; I look into the eyes of the
Master,
and thank Him that He never gave up on this old
broken vessel that has become His shining trophy.

ZION

Out of The Darkness
Into the Light

Isaiah 42:16 says, "I will lead the blind by ways they have not known, along unfamiliar paths I will guide them; I will turn the darkness into light before them and make the rough places smooth. These are the things I will do; I will not forsake them." (NIV)

The little girl sat huddled against the wall. She grabbed her legs, and put her head down in her lap. She wouldn't lift up her head. She couldn't bear to see that look of disgust in her mother's eyes. That little girl was me. The emotional pain that comes from rejection can take a lifetime to heal. That is my story of crawling out of the dark, hideous places in my life, to find redemption and wholeness with the help of a loving God. He has taken a broken, messed up individual and brought deliverance for my suffering. Relationships shape who we are as people. From our earliest memories in childhood to later in our adult years, our relationships define our lives. When those early relationships are marred with abuse, it causes us to break inside, and the result is every kind of havoc. My abuse led to years of addiction and destructive behavior.

As I share my story with you, I ask that you bear with me on the details. In order to be effective and tell my story with integrity, I must reveal things I lived through that were devastating. The stories may be gruesome at times, but they always end with purpose. When a person is broken in many different ways [as I was], her life, her decisions, her relationships, her hopes, her dreams, and everything else is impacted entirely. My hope is that from my life, and the choices I made, you will glean the tools necessary to achieve all that God has destined for you to become.

In 1984 when I accepted God's gift of grace, His Son Jesus Christ, I was given a wonderful gift to express my feelings. That gift was writing poetry, and I have shared many of them in this book. They are all signed with my pen name, Zion. They deal with many different subjects, but predominantly they speak a message of pain that was turned into deliverance and freedom.

I have also included a story told to me by my mother-in-law, Margaret Gandini, who also emerged out of darkness into the light. We shared a special bond.

Now, let us walk together through my journey. My greatest desire is that you will see yourself in my story of freedom. I believe when we are finished, you will be encouraged, and together, we can embrace the glorious future God is longing to give each and every one of us.

PART I
My Childhood/
Before Spiritual Birth

1

My Family

As with all stories, the best place to start is at the beginning. I was born in Bronx, New York, in 1951. My grandparents on my biological father's side were born in Russia and migrated to the United States to embrace the "American Dream." They were Jews by birth, but when they came to America, they stopped practicing Judaism the way they did in their homeland. They believed in order to fit in and give their future children a chance to be successful they had to leave their old religious practices behind. They no longer observed the Shabbat, which meant stopping all secular activities from Friday sundown to Saturday sundown and going to the synagogue to pray and read the Torah with other Jews who practiced Conservative Judaism. Instead, they opted for Friday night dinner with the family and whatever friends found time to come over and enjoy a night of laughter and good food. Rather than observing the traditions of Sabbath, they were satisfied to thank God as a family and say a blessing together. On the other hand, my mother's parents were first generation American Jews. I never knew my maternal grandfather; he died before I was born. My grandmother on my mother's side, or my "nanny" as I called her, was everything to me.

When I was two years old, my mother and biological father got divorced. To this day, I still don't know the real reason they split up. In fact, I have no early memory of him at all. The one redeeming factor in this mess was that I stayed in touch with his parents, my grandparents. They continued to be a great source of love and encouragement to me till the day they died. They introduced me to world of culture and artistic experiences.

After my mother divorced my biological father, she got married again to the man who would raise and adopt me as his own child. In my early years, my memory of my adopted father was a quiet, distant kind of a man who worked hard and was deeply in love with my mother. In fact, she was his childhood sweetheart. My mother's brother Jerry and my dad were childhood friends—that's how they got to know each other. After my mother's divorce, they got back in touch, and the rest is history.

We were a small family; it consisted of my adopted father, my mother, and my brother who is 3 ½ years younger than me. Early on as far back as I can remember, I saw the world differently than the rest of my family. While my parents were in a constant frenzy planning their next pretentious party and flamboyant excursions, with every designer outfit in tow, I was consumed with a desire to go to the most remote parts of the world to live and learn from people my family called "strange and weird." Not that their opinion mattered with me one hoot, but still there was the issue of money that was necessary to finance my fantasized trips. Oh, how it infuriated me that accomplishing my goals and dreams depended upon financing. Nevertheless, my parents kept a tight rein on it where I was concerned. As a result of our different points of view, an iron wall was erected in our relationship that even a demolition team could not break down.

Then there was the matter of my younger brother. He was the exact opposite of me. Despite the fact that I loved him very much, to my parents delight, he displayed a remarkable interest in achieving ways of making himself a clone of my parents. He would sit at my father's desk as a teenager, discussing such matters as pork bellies and whether the market was "bearish" or "bullish." I would stand outside, listening to these drab conversations, longing for my father's attention. Oh, yes how right my mother was when she said I was something completely different from them.

My mother was tall, thin and elegant. Her long, wavy, raven colored hair framed her peaches and cream complexion like a picture of a Madonna. When she walked by, one witnessed the epitome of femininity. She spent her time combing all the exclusive stores with friends of similar interest, and lunching at her favorite elegantly designed bistros, while strutting, her latest designer outfits. Her other interests involved more banal activities such as playing cards and Maj Jong with the girls. On the weekends my parents dined out, wearing their finest with the rest of the inner circle. Their vacations always involved going to some wonderful remote place, while my brother and I were left home with the housekeeper/babysitter. Oh, now wait a minute, I don't want you to think that they never took us anywhere. There was Niagara Falls, and winter holidays in the Catskill Mountains. But, the trips I longed to be a part of were off limits. If it sounds like I had a "chip on my shoulder," I did.

My father was not a man of the tremendous means as the rest of their group. He was a quiet man who worked from 7:00 a.m. to 12:00 p.m. six days a week to be able to give the woman he adored everything she desired. Yet, when I take stock of those days, I remember a man who was but a shadow in the background of my life in regard to my emotional needs for love and attention. Again, I don't want to mislead you. When I was sick with an inflammation of my ear drum, it was my dad who put the drops in my ear. Not to mention the times I thought I would die from pain at that "time of the month" when aspirin would not do the job. It was my dad who called the doctor and got a prescription for me to alleviate the pain. He was the most honest, hardworking man I ever knew, and I learned later in life that no man would ever love me the way he loved my mother. No, not one; EXCEPT GOD.

2

Nanny and My Younger Brother Robert

My brother was born when I was 3 ½ years old. His personality at that time was the exact opposite of mine. He was a quiet baby who put very few demands on my mother. He was so quiet he didn't speak one word till he was 5 years old. When we were little, my brother and I got along extremely well; we were quite the tag team. I remember the times we had our special moments, a "secret time," when we would take a big blanket, go under the covers together, and share our secrets. We didn't have anything that private to tell, but it was our special way of connecting with each other.

Another special person in my life was my nanny. My nanny was everything to me. She lived a couple of blocks away from my home with my mom and dad. I spent a great deal of time with her, and loved every minute of it. She was a warm, gentle soul who loved me and was not afraid to say so or show it. She was everything to me that my mother was not. To this day, I recall her sewing my party dresses from scratch. Everything she did for me was special. She loved to dress me up and put on my white ankle socks with my black patent leather Mary Jane shoes. I would parade around in my little outfits, and get up on the table and sing, "Let me entertain you." I loved being with her so much I never wanted to go home. She gave me the confidence to come out of my shell and be myself. Unlike my mother, she didn't have a problem with my creative nature or my offbeat personality. She loved me for exactly who I was. I remember her holding me when I was sick with the chicken pox. I kept asking her, "Nanny, promise me you'll never leave me, that you'll stay with me always." Of course she was not able to make that promise.

When I was 5 years old, my nanny, my best friend in the entire world, died from a stroke. That is when my world as I knew it fell apart. The unconditional love and acceptance she so freely bestowed upon me was gone. Now, I had to deal with my mother on a full time basis. Even though I loved my mother very much, she never showed me that the feelings were mutual. She was cold and distant. She had an explosive temper and very little patience for my offbeat shenanigans. I had an imaginary friend named "Magadore." I invented her to cope with my loneliness and rebellious behavior. When I acted out, such as putting my father's wallet outside the front door, or climbing up the cabinets and pulling down the dishes, I would blame Magadore as my scapegoat. She was my alter ego.

The early years of my life set the stage for what I would become later on. Already at the ripe old age of 5, I had learned that adults as far as I was concerned were unreliable and not to be trusted. Even though my adopted dad was there for me, it was my mother's lack of warmth and aloofness that left a gaping hole in my heart. Her attitude of pushing me away created in me fear, hostility, and resentment. I shut down emotionally, and became confused and unsure of how to relate to people, especially grownups.

3

Growing Up Broken

After my nanny died, when I was 5 years old, my family moved to New Rochelle, New York. Even though I felt insecure about the change, I loved the new surroundings. It was so beautiful. I enjoyed the times when our family got in the car on the weekends and went for a drive. I still can see in my mind the rolling hills, manicured lawns, big English tutor homes, and the long winding roads, which was all a new home for my vivid imagination.

My parents enrolled me in Trinity Elementary School. I still remember my kindergarten teacher, who fascinated me. She was tall, thin, and wore pretty clothes and white stockings. Her bright engaging smile made me feel excited about coming to school. Nevertheless, from the start, I had problems in school. Some of the boys teased me, and I would lash out by yelling and running out of the classroom. When I wasn't acting out, I would sit in my seat and space out. If the material didn't interest me, off I'd go in my mind to some distant place where I could run and play without any limitations. Eventually, my teacher got disgusted with my behavior and called my parents in to get their approval for the school psychologist to give me an intelligence test. She couldn't understand why I was having so many behavior problems. The test results showed an above average IQ. That didn't resolve anything. It only left everyone more confused and distrustful of me, not to mention my own confusion about why these adults were giving me such a hard time.

When I turned 11 years old, my family bought a house in Scarsdale, New York. That was the start of a life of hell and chaos that remained far too long. All I ever wanted as a kid was parents who showed me they loved and cared for me unconditionally—that unfortunately never came true. When we moved in the house, the events that transpired left me shaken to the core—my life as I knew it would never be the same. My father's mother moved in to live with us because her husband left her at 60 years old. Needless to say, she was extremely distraught and couldn't be comforted. She couldn't sleep at night, so the doctor prescribed Seconals, a highly addictive, strong sleeping pill. My mother was so disgusted with the situation that she started to fight with her constantly. I'm not just talking about verbal abuse. I remember coming home from school to find my mother beating up my grandmother. This is when my mother's addiction to pills began. She started taking the sleeping pills away from my grandmother and taking them herself. What a nightmare it was for me to come home to a house where there was constant instability and violence! I had no clue how to handle any of this insanity. My father would come home from work, witness what was happening with the fights; then he'd turn to me, an 11 year old child, and ask me how he should deal with the situation. My life was consumed with fear. As a result of my mother's growing addiction, her behavior became cruel towards me, and I was left to fend for myself. I remember times when she would be so over medicated on the pills that she would call me into her bedroom, demanding that I make her tea. When I brought it upstairs to her, if it wasn't made according to her specifications, she would yell and scream at me to do it over again. It was at this stage that I started to act out. I felt so alone and desperately longed for someone to show me that my life mattered. I was determined to get attention, even if it meant punishment. I resorted to going into Macy's Department Store and stealing whatever I could shove into my pocketbook. The store detectives spotted me, and dragged me into a big, dark, concrete walled room, demanding an explanation for my behavior. Since, I didn't want to give them an answer as to why I was stealing, they made me give them my parent's phone number so they could come and get me. When they showed up, they were extremely angry with me. I gave them a nonchalant shrug off my shoulders, never offering a single word of apology. I was 11 years old when this happened.

After 1 year of that madness, my grandmother was committed to a mental institution where she was given constant rounds of shock treatments. She never got out of that hospital. From what I was told, she died of a heart attack and I never saw her again.

My parents sold the house; we rented an apartment and moved back to New Rochelle. Needless to say, I was extremely happy to get out of that hellish environment. At this point in my young life, I was an insecure, frightened, miserable child getting ready to embark upon my teenage years.

When we moved back to New Rochelle I was excited about starting Junior High School. I was desperate to make friends and find people I could connect with. I thought that finally the nightmare and the misery from the events in the house in Scarsdale were behind me. Unfortunately, that dream was anything but my reality. Shortly after moving into our new apartment, my mother's addiction to the sleeping pills was still in full force. I'd come home from school to find my father in a frenzy. My mother was driving to different doctors in Manhattan to get these sleeping pills. Her behavior was causing my father to become desperate to find a solution for her destructive behavior. I'd come home from school and find my dad crying because he didn't know how to get her to stop hurting herself. He would insist that I accompany him on the rounds to find my mother's pill bottles. I felt like a Saint Bernard dog sniffing out the contraband. It was devastating and frightening for me to deal with my mother's addition. My life at home with all the problems left me feeling hopeless. I would often say, "Dawn, you'd be better off if you were never born. If I was a better kid, my mother wouldn't have these problems." I blamed myself for my mother's condition.

Things finally came to a horrendous head. On a sunny beautiful day that felt like nothing could go wrong, everything fell apart. My father got a call from the police stating that my mother had a car accident and was taken to New Rochelle Hospital. She was driving back from New York City after getting a prescription for the sleeping pills from one of her doctors. She fell asleep at the wheel, crashed the car, then went through the windshield and wound up in the emergency room. To this day the image of my mother in a white gown sitting in that stark room with blood gushing from her face still haunts me. Even though I was horrified, I wanted desperately to hold her and tell her everything is going to be alright. Unfortunately, I could only see her from outside of the room, I wasn't allowed to go in.

Thankfully, after that incident, my mother went for psychological help and stopped taking the sleeping pills. Instead, due to her anxiety and depression, she was given tranquilizers. Her destructive behavior had taken a toll on my father and me. Oddly enough, my brother was unaware and protected from the gory details of her behavior and what had transpired in our household. It was always my father and I who had to pick up the pieces and move on. My reaction to all of this instability was total confusion; I never knew what to expect, or what was going to happen next. On the outside, if you met me, I appeared to be a confident, happy go lucky, young girl excited about life. On the inside, I was totally broken.

4

Abuse/Addiction

When I was 14 my parents allowed me to date. One of the few positive things my mother said to me was, "You are very pretty, even prettier than I was at your age; make sure you take advantage of your good looks." She never complimented me on my character or personality; to her, being a good looking girl was all that mattered. Nevertheless, I took the positive reinforcement to heart. I was so desperate for her approval that I was willing to do anything to please her, no matter what it was. Since I was feeling fairly confident about myself on the surface, dating was something I was really excited about. I basked in the attention the guys showered upon me. In their company, I felt valued, and appreciated. I would love to spend hours getting ready for my dates. After all, they were bombarding me with attention that I wasn't receiving at home.

During this time, my mother's mood swings toward me were very severe. On the one hand, we would have girls' night together; that included playing jacks on the floor, watching beauty contests, and shopping for clothes—then on the other hand there were the days where she would snap verbally by yelling and smacking me for no reason. My life at home with my mother was an out of control merry-go-round ride, never knowing what she was going to do next, or how she was going to react to me. One of the things that really hurt me was that my father would never intervene nor say anything to her about abusing me. He was afraid to confront her about her mood swings. His motto was, "Keep the peace at all costs." The thing that made it even more confusing for me was the times when I went to my girlfriend's houses, their mothers would welcome me with open arms and show me the attention I never received at home. I just couldn't understand why they were so warm and friendly toward me, and my own mother treated me like I was her worst enemy.

There was one particular incident of physical abuse that hurt me to the core. My mother was supposed to drive me to my girlfriend's house since she needed her car to run errands. I was standing in her bedroom near her closet talking to her while she was looking for an outfit to wear. She turned around, and looked at me with eyes of hatred and said, "You're so much more beautiful than I am." When she said this to me, I had no idea where she was coming from. All I was thinking about was getting a ride to my friend's house. I did nothing to provoke her. My response to her was, "Mom, don't say that. You're much more beautiful than I could ever be." She got infuriated. She turned around and slapped me across my face so hard that my head shook. I was so petrified that I ran away from her into the living room. She came charging at me as if she wanted to kill me. I locked myself in the bathroom. She stood outside the bathroom door and commanded me to open the door. I knew if I opened the door she was going to hurt me. My response was, "I'm not opening this door, I didn't do anything to you, and you smacked me for nothing." She promised me if

I opened the door she wouldn't hit me. I opened the door and she came charging at me with both hands extended reaching toward my face. She took her nails and dug them into my eyebrows. To this day, I still have a scar over the eyebrow where she attacked me. I ran out of the house, took a train to Manhattan to my biological grandfather's office. I told him what had happened and he tried his best to calm me down. What really hurt me was that he called my mother and father and told them I was with him. I desperately wanted him to let me stay there since I felt safe with him. My parents came down to Manhattan to pick me up. My mother never apologized, and no one ever mentioned the incident again. This was just one of the many examples of the physical abuse my mother perpetrated upon me. She was extremely violent towards me, and anything could set her off. Still, I would never hit her back. There was one time when she was hitting me with a belt; I was so scared that I pushed her backwards very hard. If I hadn't defended myself, I knew she could have damaged me permanently. I think what hurt me more than even the physical abuse was the times that she told me she hated me and wished I was never born. The physical abuse I was able to overcome, but it was her words of rejection that did the real damage. It wasn't until I was older that I came to understand that hurting people hurt people. She once told me that when she was a child her father would hit her for no reason. That's all the detail she gave me, and I wouldn't dare ask her any more questions.

It is very important to me that you understand that my motives for sharing the abuse with you is by no means to make my mother out to be a monster. I've come to understand that she had deep rooted mental issues that caused her to do these things to me. She didn't have a clue how to control her urges of violence that came from a place that even she didn't understand.

ABUSE/ADDICTION

In those days, therapy wasn't what it is today. Unfortunately, back then people would shove issues like abuse under the table, and not discuss them. There were times when she treated me wonderfully. For example, on my 16th birthday she planned a costume party for me and told me to invite all my friends. It was last minute, but all my friends showed up in costumes, and we enjoyed the lunch and birthday cake my mother made. My friends couldn't say enough about the wonderful day they had.

One thing that plagued me every month was my menstrual cycle. During the first and second day, I would experience excruciating pain. When aspirin didn't help, my father would call the family doctor and ask him for a prescription of painkillers for me. At the time he thought he was helping me. When I took percocet [a strong narcotic] for the first time, it made me so dizzy, I felt like I was walking through a dark tunnel that was swallowing me up. If I had even the least bit of common sense I would have realized that this drug was something I should never put in my mouth again. Yet, in spite of the horrible reaction I experienced from taking these pills, I didn't stop. When I took them, they not only alleviated my physical pain, but they blocked out all the emotional pain, leaving me numb; I didn't have to deal with anything at all. At first I only took the pills when I had my period, but eventually I started taking them at the slightest provocation of pain. Whenever I could get my hands on them, I would take them. After awhile, I built up a tolerance towards them. When I took them, they created the false illusion in me that I could handle anything with ease. I knew in my mind that these pills were like picking up a deadly serpent that had the poison to potentially kill me, but I didn't care.

On the outside, my high school years looked very promising. I had developed many friendships that I built my world around. I did well in school most of the time, but my main focus was the time I spent with the friends who accepted and appreciated me. What I didn't realize at the time was that these people were incapable of filling the brokenness and loneliness in my heart. It became a vicious cycle striving to get acceptance from people. It never worked; when I didn't get it the way I wanted it, I felt crushed and empty.

Finally, the day came when I was able to leave home to go to college. The year was 1969, the world was changing drastically and these were exciting times to be alive in. I was thrilled to get away from home and be on my own with no limits imposed upon me. I picked a junior college in Boston, since Boston is a college town that's loaded with great universities. Things were heating up in those days politically and the students were speaking out against the Viet Nam War, which I was in strong opposition to. As soon as I arrived at school I got settled in my dormitory and made friends with two girls who were also from New York.

Since I grew up during the hippie generation, my motto along with many others during that time was that life was about drugs, sex, and rock and roll; that was the culture. Instead of focusing on getting a good education, once again my priority was making friends, dating and having a good time. The political climate at the time was charged with activists who were standing up and speaking out for change in the old value systems which we believed no longer applied to our generation. We were rebelling, and thought it was no longer relevant to adhere to the moral values our parents tried to impose on us. We considered ourselves a new breed of young people that stood for love, peace and equality between the sexes. These were turbulent times where young people were running around to and fro like chickens without a head, screaming for freedom from

ABUSE/ADDICTION

the old system of conformity. We were part of the counter-culture that wanted to drop out and turn on. We were experimenting with all kinds of drugs such as pot, LSD and various other hallucinogens. I started smoking pot and before I knew it, my addictive personality was rearing its ugly head. My declaration to myself was, "Others were doing it, so why shouldn't I?" What I didn't realize was that they were just experimenting with the drugs, but I had an addictive personality that pot alone couldn't satisfy. I needed much more than pot to disguise my feelings and satisfy my insecurities.

My drug usage at college started me on a downward spiral, and I found myself losing control. I started taking "uppers" [speed] from one of my friends in my dorm. Her father was a doctor and gave her amphetamines for a weight problem. She offered the pills to me one night when we were staying up all night to cram for midterms. As soon as I took them and felt that euphoric sensation, I knew I was in love and never wanted to be without them. They made me feel courageous—as if I was unstoppable. These dangerous pills gave me a false sense of confidence; even though I would crash and burn when I came down from them, I didn't care. Since she didn't like them, I was glad to take them off her hands. Not only was I taking them to cram for exams, but I started taking them whenever I could get my hands on them. Eventually, one pill wasn't doing it for me. When I knew she was going out, since we didn't have locks on our doors, I would slip into her room, go into her drawer where the pills were, and pour out a handful, close the drawer as if nothing happened and rush to my room. Alone at last with my beloved pills, I would swallow two, and then an hour later, take a third one. I hated myself for being so sneaky, not to mention taking advantage of my friend's trust, but I wanted the pills so badly, I threw all reason to the wind. After awhile she started noticing the negative effects they were having on my personality, and she didn't want to give them to me anymore. I wouldn't take no for an answer. I offered her money for the pills, but she refused. After that incident, I got scared and decided to back off, knowing if I continued taking them from her, I could wind up being kicked out of school. Or, worse yet, have the school call my parents, and face my mother's wrath. The pitiful thing about the whole mess was that I was so blinded by the high I refused to look at the handwriting on the wall that was screaming YOU'RE BECOMING AN ADDICT! The last thing I wanted to admit was that I might have a drug problem like my mother.

After one year at Grahm Junior College, my 2 best friends decided to transfer to Miami University. Of course, I wanted to transfer there too. My parents' answer to my request to transfer schools was, "Absolutely not." They said that Miami University was a party school and they weren't going to pay for me to spend my days on the beach. Feeling defeated by my parents refusal, I decided to apply to Monmouth College in New Jersey and was accepted. Once again I felt powerless to stand up to my parents and reacted with anger and hostility. Since I wasn't allowed to go to the school I wanted, I rebelled and my attitude became—I don't care what happens. My priority was my friends and not an education, so it no longer mattered to me where I went to school. Looking back, I realize how foolish I was to give up my opportunity to get a good education. My distorted view of reality had me thinking that without my friends, life had no meaning.

I went to Monmouth for one semester and flunked out. In my rebellion I hardly ever showed up for class, and when I did I was either late or high. It wasn't that I didn't want to learn; the truth was that I was so screwed up from suppressing all the hurt and pain in my childhood due the abuse I didn't have a clue how to set goals and be successful. I had no idea of what I wanted to do or be in life. The only information I had to go on was that my parents wanted me to find a rich prospect for a husband; someone who would take care of me for the rest of my life. Not that their attitude was so terrible; most parents want their daughters to have financial security, but what I really needed was professional help to overcome the pain that caused my rebellion in the first place. With my distorted view of myself and the world, I didn't have a chance to do anything positive with my life. The world to me was a scary place filled only with gloom and doom. I saw everything and everyone from a place of fear and distrust. Even though I had so much to be grateful for, I was so broken on the inside I didn't believe I deserved anything good.

After flunking out of Monmouth College, my only option was to move back home with my parents and find a job. Because of all my wrong choices, my life was taking a turn for the worse, and I knew I had to make some tough decisions. In my heart I had dreamed of doing something meaningful with my life and helping people; yet I would ask myself, "How can you help anybody else when you're was so screwed up that you can't even help yourself?" So, I moved back in with my parents. I knew I had to give up the pills, but I didn't believe I could function without them. I was so crippled by the emotional pain of my failures, when I would think about it I'd feel like a knife was sticking in my stomach. So, here I was 20 years old, back at home with mommy and daddy without a clue of how to make my life work. Without much trouble, I landed a job in the garment district in New York City. I liked making my own money, but I was really bored with the job and frustrated with living at home. The only excitement I had was my boyfriend who was in the Marines. We had met in Florida during my spring break when I was at Grahm Junior College. He was in boot camp for training, and back then the only way we could communicate was by mail and occasional phones calls. We didn't have all the goodies we have today such as E-mail, texting, or Skype. He was a great guy who respected me and wasn't afraid to show me he cared. When he got out of boot camp, I knew he was serious about our relationship and wanted to take it to another level. Yet, in my insecurity and desperation for my mother's approval, I broke it off. She had expressed to me her disapproval since he was not in college pursuing a high paying career. So, I did what I always did back then—find some way to destroy anything that would incur my mother's wrath and rejection. I was so screwed up I didn't realize that no matter what I did, I would never get her approval.

After breaking up with him I later regretted it, even though I knew I had no hope of making him happy in the condition I was in. I kept asking myself, "How can you make someone else happy when you're so self-destructive?" After this relationship, I resorted to taking pills again—my way of dealing with hurt, pain and failure. Once again I gave up on myself. I knew I needed help, but I was too frightened to reveal my addiction to my parents.

Besides taking pills, my other form of escape was getting involved in relationships that I knew wouldn't work out. In my heart I was desperate for love and wanted badly to have a relationship with someone who would love and value me. Yet in my head was that voice telling me, "If your parents don't love you, what makes you think that you're worthy of being loved?" After two more failed relationships, I decided it was time to move out of my parents' house and be on my own. I moved to Manhattan, rented an apartment and got a new job.

ABUSE/ADDICTION

When I wasn't working, I was making the rounds to doctors complaining that I had extreme menstrual pain. Of course, my motives were to get my drug of choice, percocet. This pill is a strong narcotic that's a controlled substance and it's generally prescribed to cancer patients or patients with serious illnesses. Before I knew it, I was taking 30 pills a day. I'd take 8 in the morning before going to work; then come back home and take the rest. It's still a mystery to me that I was able to work and function. On the weekends my only interest was taking the pills and passing out. I was so disappointed in myself, I stop caring about my life and the dreams I had as a child. I spent all of my free time alone in my apartment taking pills and watching television. After awhile I didn't even enjoy the high. My only desire was to kill the feelings I couldn't control. Looking back on my actions, I realize my rebellion and addiction was my way of trying to punish my parents, namely my mother. What was so ironic was that they were enjoying their life, while I was punishing myself for the abuse that wasn't my fault.

This behavior went on for a couple of years. Eventually, my parents found out about my drug abuse and insisted I go to rehab. After much prompting, I took their suggestion and entered a rehab that offered both detox and rehabilitation. I hated every minute of it, and after the detox was over, I left. I was so deceived, I thought that I could go back to life as usual and everything would be fine. What I failed to understand was that there was no such thing as life as usual for me. I was still an addict who had no idea of how to live life as a healthy individual. I was still running from all the brokenness inside of me, not to mention the intense fear of facing the demons that held me captive. So, I kept on running and kept on taking pills. This was taking such a tremendous toll on my physical and mental health that I was no longer capable of keeping a job. I had lost so many opportunities with great companies because of my addiction.

Finally, my pill addiction got so terrible I had to check into a local hospital. They started giving me methadone to get off the pills. I had never even heard of this drug prior to going into the hospital. I later found out this is the same poison they give to heroin addicts. They claimed since percocet is such a strong narcotic, and I was popping 30 of these a day, this was their only option to detoxify me. The problem with this method of detox was that the methadone was so much more powerful than the percocet, it had me walking around like a zombie. I wandered around the hospital ward for 3 weeks stoned out of my mind; I didn't even know where I was at the time. Before I left, they gave me the worst advice I'd ever received from a health care professional. They advised me to get into a methadone maintenance program. According to them, this would be an opportunity for me to work and function. Since I was living alone with no advice from anyone, I went ahead and did what they suggested. You would think that a light bulb would have gone off in my brain telling me, "If you take their advice you'll be digging even into a deeper pit of destruction for yourself." Little did I know at the time that this medication would cause my life to completely fall apart. I was getting rid of one drug, only to start a whole new chapter with another one. The help I so desperately needed was not drug related. I felt so hopeless at this point that I no longer cared if I lived or died. So, began the complete downward spiral of going everyday to the methadone program and hanging around with people that had also given up on life. With these people I felt accepted, since they made no demands on me to change. I rarely ever communicated with my parents and friends any more. I found myself totally immersed in a subculture of people who were doing nothing and

ABUSE/ADDICTION

going nowhere but down. This lifestyle lasted approximately 4 years. Not only was I taking the methadone, but after that high waned and my body built up a tolerance, I started abusing tranquilizers with the methadone. There were times when I was so out of it, I'd overdose from the pills, wind up in the emergency room, and barely make it out alive. I'm still amazed that I didn't die from the excessive amount of times I winded up in the hospital from an overdose. I recall one particular time I overdosed so badly they had to put a tube down my throat to prevent me from choking on my own vomit. Insanely enough, I got out of the hospital and went right back to the same behavior. If it wasn't for God protecting my life, I wouldn't be here writing my testimony to you.

I remember the day I finally said, "Enough is enough." I woke up, looked at the sink filled with dirt and crust, my clothes thrown everywhere, bugs crawling on the walls, and said; "That's it. I can't do this anymore. I have to get help." I remembered an advertisement I'd seen for a long-term rehabilitation program called Daytop Village. They were located in Manhattan where I was living at the time. I called them up, told them my situation and to my amazement they told me someone had cancelled that day, and if I wanted the spot, I had to get there no later than 8:00 p.m. I took a couple of large black garbage bags, stuffed my clothes in, left the apartment and took a taxi downtown to the Induction Center. When I arrived, they put me through a very intense interview to make sure I was willing to commit to the treatment program till the end, which on average was 1 ½ to 2 years. I was so desperate and disgusted with myself; I decided I would do whatever it took to graduate. I spent approximately 1 ½ years in Daytop Village which was located in Swan Lake, New York. It was a beautiful facility which housed approximately 150 residents.

During my time there, I attended group sessions, confrontation groups, groups that lasted 3 days with little to no sleep, and other forms of treatment that were very intense. For the first time, I was forced to look at myself honestly, and was held accountable for my behavior. Without the drugs to mask the pain, my emotions were exposed, and I had to take a good hard look at what had brought me to this point in my life.

While I was in Daytop, I made a lot of good friends; these were people who genuinely cared about me. I came to realize that when I wasn't high or drugged, people liked me, and miracle of all miracles, I even liked myself. This was the first time I was clean and sober since I was 18 years old. I was 27 when I entered Daytop, and I had been getting high from one drug or another approximately 10 years straight. Even though I stayed in the program and participated with the treatment, I still found it extremely hard to open up to people and share my feelings. I had covered up my pain for such a long time that facing it, and dealing with it, was an excruciating process. In order for me to move forward, I had to accept the wrong choices I made, and the consequences that resulted from those choices.

While there, every resident had to abide by the rules and regulations they set for us during our time in treatment. One of rules they strictly enforced was that residents were forbidden to get involved in sexual relationships. They believed it would distract us from focusing on our treatment. However, we were permitted in the last phase of our treatment (Phase B), to pursue these relationships with other residents. From the time I arrived upstate there was one particular guy who caught my eye. We had developed a close friendship, and we had many things in common. What attracted me to him most of all was his wit, intelligence and creativity. We developed an

ABUSE/ADDICTION

honest relationship and I knew I could count on him for support and encouragement. While we were upstate, we abided by the rules and never stepped out of the boundaries they set. We both entered the final phase of our treatment at the same time. In Phase B, it was our responsibility to go to work and save money to move out. During that time, we spent a lot of quality time together, and decided we wanted to take the relationship to the next level. I had found a job with an international shipping company, and I was so grateful to be clean and working. My nights consisted of long walks and intimate talks with my best friend. He always knew how to surprise me, taking me to quaint little restaurants, Central Park, and out of the way places in the City that I'd never been before. We realized we were falling in love. These new emotions made me very excited, yet scared at the same time. I was asking myself, "Am I ready for this? Have I worked on myself enough to trust him with my heart?" He had been working for 9 months and finally saved enough money to rent a studio apartment. After he got settled in his new apartment, he called me one evening and asked me to move in with him. Originally, my plan was to share an apartment with one of my girlfriends from treatment who had also moved out. I didn't want to disappoint her, but on the other hand, I certainly didn't want to miss out on the chance that this relationship would work out and turn into something permanent. After all, we were getting together for all the right reasons; we were both clean and sober, we loved to be together, and we had the same goals. So, I decided to take the risk and go for it.

For the first time in my life I felt a sense of happiness and contentment. I was not only drug free but in love. I thought things couldn't get any better; I had a great job, lots of close friends, communication with my family, and self respect for the first time in my life. On the outside everything looked perfect, and for 2 years it was. Our lives together consisted of working hard, going on vacations, and doing whatever we could to reach out to our community. Even though everything seemed perfect, there came a point when the stresses and demands of everyday life took a toll on me. I was still struggling with temptation and other debilitating emotions that were rearing their ugly head. Even though I had graduated from treatment at Daytop, I still had issues with self esteem that a love relationship couldn't fix. There were times when I would feel despair and depression for no reason. I started to realize that I still had many layers of emotional pain that I had not dealt with in treatment. When I got out of Daytop, I was so excited with my new life that I didn't recognize the subtle hints that were surfacing from time to time. Because of the huge hole in my heart from the abuse in my childhood, I still believed I was unworthy of happiness. Whenever I made the slightest mistake, I would condemn myself for not being stronger or smarter. My other mistake was not continuing my therapy after Daytop. I was so desperate to be successful after years of failure that I didn't want to admit to myself or others that I still had these unresolved emotions, and still needed help. I would hear those old messages in my head from my childhood that said, "No matter what goes on in your life, you have to look good, sound good, and be successful in everything you do—there is no room for failure." The problem with these messages that resounded so loudly was that I was listening to false information that appeared true.

After struggling with these feelings for months, I succumbed to the temptation and made an appointment with my gynecologist to get pain killers. I deceived myself into believing, "I'll do it one time, and it won't hurt me." How could I have been so blind not to realize that I was picking up the very

ABUSE/ADDICTION

thing that took me down!! After taking the first pill, there were immediate consequences—one pill wasn't enough. So, here I was taking 4-5 pills at one time. That is the insanity and vicious cycle of addiction; it's a progressive disease. As they say in Narcotics Anonymous, "You pick up one time, and the addiction starts all over again." They also say, "The definition of insanity is to think you can do the same crazy thing over again and expect different results." This not only applies to drugs, it also applies to any addiction whether it's food, sex, gambling, and the list goes on and on. In order to be free, the root of the addiction has to be faced head on. Once the addiction is acknowledged, the thinking patterns must change. If the root of the addiction is not addressed, it will never cease to be a source of destruction. I realized I had only scratched the surface in dealing with my issues that caused my addiction. I still had to go deeper to find out what I needed to do to recover once and for all.

Once I started using again, I found out my boyfriend was also taking drugs. Since I was back to my old ways of making the rounds to doctors for the percocet, and consuming in a matter of months, 20 pills a day, Chris started to suspect that I had picked up again. He confronted me on it, and I immediately confessed to him the struggles I had been experiencing emotionally, and that I had succumbed to the temptation to get high. When he saw how broken I was over it, he started to cry, and confessed to me that he had been struggling and was also trapped in the vicious web of addiction. Now that the cat was out of the bag, we both said, "What the hell," and started to get high together. He would shoot his heroin, and I would swallow my pills. This lasted only a couple of months when finally we had a close call that almost led to Chris dying of an overdose. That day, Chris took me down to the lower east side of Manhattan. He told me he was going to buy a few bags of heroin. I was petrified at his suggestion; I had always been afraid of heroin since I heard of so many deaths related to it. I told him, "I don't want to take that poison, and I don't want you to take it either." He told me, "You don't have to shoot it up, you can snort it." Even though I really didn't want to take it, there was something on the inside of me that was excited at the prospect of scoring heroin with him and trying it for the first time. Without much trouble, he was able to score 6 bags for $60; the dealer told us this was supposed to be the good stuff. Once we were done with the dealer, we got on the train heading for home to get high on the heroin. When we walked in the house, Chris went into the bathroom to put the heroin in the needle. I waited in the living room till he came out to give me my share. When he walked into the living room, he handed me 3 bags and told me, "Dawn, don't get scared when I put the needle in my arm, the blood is going to come up and I might start nodding out." I sat there on pins and needles watching him since I had never seen anyone put a needle in their arm. After he shot the drugs into his vein, he fell backwards and started to groan. In less than a minute, he passed out and I was left alone with him while he went into an overdose. I started to freak out. I was screaming and shaking him. "Chris, wake up!" I got no response. I started panicking, since I didn't know what to do to get him to respond. I wanted to put him in the shower, but there was no way I would be able to lift him up. In a state of frenzy, I called 911. I told them the situation and they said, "We'll be right there." While I waited for them to come, I pulled the needle out of his arm, took the bags of dope, and hid them. Even though I was scared that they might search for the drugs, I still wanted to take my share. How insane was I? My boyfriend had just overdosed on

ABUSE/ADDICTION

heroin, and my thinking was, "I still want to take my share!" After a couple of minutes, the ambulance came with 2 police officers. They confronted me on what had happened, and I told them, "My boyfriend just overdosed by accident." They looked at me suspiciously, but were more concerned with getting Chris to the hospital at that moment than pursuing the details with me. I rode in the ambulance while the medical technicians put an IV into Chris' arm. I sat there in a state of shock trying to understand how we had gotten to this point. When we arrived at the hospital, the nurses were waiting for us since the EMT people had called ahead. They only asked me one question, "How long has he been out?" With my lips quivering, I answered, "About a half hour." They put him on a stretcher and rushed him inside the emergency room. They wouldn't let me go with them, so I sat down with my head in my hands consumed with fear and disgust. After about 15 minutes, one of the nurses came out and told me, "He's going to make it—if he had gotten here a couple of minutes later, he would have died." I asked if I could see him, and they escorted me back to the room where he was staying. When I saw him, I burst into tears and told him, "Chris, I could have lost you." He told me he was alright and that I should go home by cab, and when they released him, he would come back home. I kissed him goodbye while expressing to him my relief that he's going to okay. I took a cab back to Brooklyn shaking from the event that had just transpired. I was so overwhelmed; I rationalized to myself, "After what you've been through, you need the drugs to calm down." That's the insane mind of an addict! I went to where they were hidden and took out what was left of the heroin. I didn't know how much to take since I had never taken heroin before. I decided to snort one bag, and see what happened. After I had consumed the entire bag, I experienced a high like no other high I had ever had. It felt like my body was consumed by a heat that penetrated my entire being. I was so stoned, I started to nod out. I don't know how long I was in that state when Chris walked into the house. He saw me in that condition, but since he was still stoned from all the drugs, even though they had revived him, he went into the bedroom and got lost in his own world. We spent the rest of the evening both stoned, lost in our drug induced insanity. The next morning we woke up, mentioned it briefly and that was the end of it. I took the rest of the heroin that I had hidden and flushed it down the toilet. I knew after that incident I was never going to take that fatal drug again.

Crazy as it was, I continued using the percocet. On the outside, you'd never know Chris and I were had started taking drugs again—we were still working and taking care of all of our responsibilities. That's one of the dangers of addiction—you can get by for awhile until eventually, everything spirals out of control. We were able to keep up the illusion of success which addicts tend to do in the beginning, but as with anything destructive, it eventually catches up with you. Since we were at that point, we realized we had to do something different. I suggested we move out of New York and start over in another state. I was so ashamed of my failure; I didn't want to face my friends and family. I hated to leave New York, the only home I ever knew, but at that point I didn't have a solution for us. In spite of us turning back to drugs, I still loved Chris and wanted this relationship to work out. He agreed to my suggestion and went to stay temporarily with his brother in Kansas while I finished up last minute details in New York. I sold the furniture, drained my bank account, and flew to Kansas to start our new journey. We bought a used car and decided to travel from Kansas to Colorado. When we got to Colorado, the beauty intrigued us, so we make a decision to rent an apartment and try to make things work. Chris immediately got a job working for the best antique dealer in Denver. It wasn't difficult for him to get hired since he had developed a very extensive portfolio while working in New York. I had a lot of difficulty finding a job in my profession as a legal secretary. My fast talking New York ways did not endear me with the people who interviewed me. Compared to New York, Colorado is a laid back, low key place. Eventually, I got a job working for two Jewish transplanted New York attorneys. Chris and I settled into our new apartment, reported every day to our new jobs, explored the beautiful snowcapped Colorado Mountains, and tried to reinvent ourselves in this new environment. We adjusted and enjoyed our new found life, but only for a short time. We had moved to a new location, but we brought with us all the unresolved issues that had led us back into addiction. I remember the night we were invited to a party with some of our new friends. From the moment I walked in the door, I didn't like the scene. In one room the people were smoking pot—the smoke was so thick and blinding I couldn't see in front of me. The sweet aroma of the marijuana was so intense it was making me nauseas. In another room people were sitting on the floor snorting cocaine on a cracked mirror. My mind was in a whirlwind and I knew this whole scene spelled DANGER. I was frantically looking for my boyfriend when suddenly I heard his voice laughing behind the bathroom door. I knocked, but he didn't respond. I sensed that he didn't want to let me in. I insisted, and when he opened the door and I got into the room, I was horrified. There he was with another guy shooting cocaine into his veins. I knew right then and there that even though we had changed our environment by moving to Denver, we were about to spiral downward into a deep dark hole. I loved him very much, and didn't want to believe or accept that this relationship was going down the drain. It's really hard for two addicts, or recovering addicts, to stay together and remain straight. Once again, I felt lost, scared, and overwhelmed.

When we got back home, I tried getting past the pain and disappointment of what was happening. I knew we were not going to make it together. If we continued doing drugs we would have wound up totally destroying each other. I decided I had to go back to New York without him. That was probably one of the most painful and difficult decisions I had ever made. Even though we were not good for each other, I really loved him. There was only one positive that came out of this failed relationship; God used our breakup to reveal Himself to me and change my life for good.

Now, that I've shared with you the brokenness and misery in my life, it's time to walk out of the darkness into His marvelous Light. My heart's desire is that you will continue to walk with me on my life's changing journey.

PART II
Meeting Christ/ Spiritual Birth

5

Revelation—God's Call

The word "Revelation" means an uncovering, a removal of the veil; a disclosure of what was previously hidden or unknown. When God reveals Himself to an individual, in essence what he is doing is making Himself known personally in order to develop a relationship with that person. He does that in many different ways. He can do it through personal revelation such as dreams and visions as He did with the Prophet Daniel (Daniel 2:19-23). Another way God gets people's attention is through other believers who share their faith with them (Romans 10:17).

In my case, God made Himself known to me personally—He also used people to share the Gospel [the good news about Jesus Christ] with me. When I got back to New York from Colorado, I was devastated over the breakup with my boyfriend. I went to live with one of my girlfriends and got a job working in my profession as a legal assistant. It took all the strength I could muster up to get through the day at work. Looking back, there was one day in particular that stands out where God was trying to get my attention. It was 5:00 p.m., the end of the work day. I went into the bathroom and started to cry. The emotional pain from missing Chris was so intense that I felt like waves of anguish were pulsing throughout my entire body. I could hardly get myself together enough to leave the bathroom. Finally, I put on a fake smile and said goodnight to my fellow co-workers and left the office. When I walked into the street, I felt so detached emotionally I was having trouble relating to my surroundings. I could hear the noise from the traffic and see the people scurrying about their business, but it felt like it was coming from a distant place way out yonder. I was so overwhelmed by the gripping emotional pain inside that I totally lost my bearings. I felt the panic starting to choke me. In my mind I screamed out, "Now, what am I going to do with my life?" An answer came back to me with such clarity that it shocked me. The voice in mind said, "Call Jews for Jesus." At this point, I thought I was going crazy. I screamed back to myself, "I'm a Jew! Why would I call Jews for Jesus?" Making every effort to get my mind together, to my amazement, I heard again, "Call Jews for Jesus" as clear as a bell. After hearing it the second time, I started to wonder what it meant, and what I should do about it. I searched my memory bank for any recollection I might have regarding Jews for Jesus. To my surprise, I recalled an incident many years prior. I was walking out of a subway car on my way to work when a person handed me a track from Jews for Jesus. At the time, it made me very angry; I threw the track on the floor, and shouted to the person who gave it to me, "I'm a Jew, I don't believe in Jesus." Again, I wondered, what does all this mean? At the time while all this was going on in my head, I was standing in front of a pay phone. I decided; let me call information and see if there is a listing for Jews for Jesus. I was surprised when the operator gave me their phone number. I decided to take a chance and give them a call. When I called, a very sweet, unpretentious voice got on the phone saying, "Good afternoon, this is Jews for Jesus, how can I be of service to you?" I froze. I didn't know what to say, or how to respond. I was still wondering, "Who or what was that voice in my head that told me to call this organization?" They really do exist! Without much prompting, I found myself sharing my story about my unhappiness since I left my boyfriend in Colorado. I also told her about the voice in my head telling me to call Jews for Jesus. I remember her gentle chuckle. She responded as if she had some inside information I didn't have. She asked me where I was calling from so I gave told her my address. I was shocked to find out they were only a 10 minute cab ride away. She asked me, "Could you please come over here as soon as possible? We have people who would love to talk to you." As outlandish as this whole experience seemed to me, I was drawn to it, and wanted to find out more.

I took a cab to the West Side of Manhattan and went upstairs. There was a delightful, engaging woman at the front desk who told me to come in. She asked me who I was, and when I told her, she responded as if she had known me for a long time. As I took a quick glimpse of the office, I noticed quite a few young people engaging in pleasant, carefree conversation. I thought to myself, "Why do these people look as if they're on cloud nine?" The whole thing seemed unreal, and the people looked like a bunch of flakes to me. Since I was feeling so lonely and unhappy, it was really hard for me to believe that these people could truly be this happy and upbeat. I was so filled with skepticism, it clouded my mind from believing in the hope they exuded. Almost instantly, I was ushered into one of their back offices. I was greeted by a trio of people who looked at me like I was one of their long lost relatives. In spite of my obvious annoyance, they calmly asked me how they could be of assistance. Despite my distrust, again I found myself opening up and relating to them what I had been going through. I told them I was Jewish, that I had left my boyfriend in Colorado who meant the world to me, and I'm here because I just had the strangest experience. I went on about the voice that told me to call their organization. Just like the woman I initially spoke to on the phone, there was a smile and look of acknowledgement on their faces. They told me they were also Jews and they believed from what I shared with them that God was trying to get my attention. I was very surprised to learn that these people had similar stories of encounters with God—if in fact that was what I was experiencing. Even though the whole thing seemed unreal to me, they had my undivided attention. As I listened to their stories, something inside of me was coming alive. When they asked if they could pray with me, I gladly consented. Afterwards, they offered to drive me back to Brooklyn where I was staying. I still couldn't understand why these strangers were so accommodating to me. I knew one thing from this experience; they had something that I didn't, and that was peace.

When I got home, I told my girlfriend the experience I had with the people at Jews for Jesus. She quickly dismissed it and, for the time being, so did I. As the days went on, I slipped into a deep, dark depression. No matter how hard I tried, I couldn't find any reason to believe that things were going to get better. Once again, I turned to pills to soothe the nagging pain. Little did I know at that time that God was waiting right around the corner to bring in the reinforcements I needed to take me out of the hell I had created for myself.

It was a Sunday afternoon. Since I wasn't working that day, I decided to go into Manhattan. I was so out of it that I was wandering around the streets like a homeless vagabond. It was a cold, bleak winter day; it matched perfectly with what I was feeling. After hours of walking aimlessly, I went into a coffee shop across from Madison Square Garden. What happened in that coffee show is forever etched in my memory. While I sipped my coffee and ate my donut with my head almost in the plate; I noticed out of the corner of my eye a woman approaching me joined by a group of other women in the background. She walked right up to me, and said, "Jesus loves you." At first, I thought I was hearing things. I didn't look up or, answer her. Again, she looked down at me, and said, "God sent me into this coffee shop to let you know that Jesus loves you." She didn't stop there; she went on to say more. She said, "I am an evangelist and singer. My ministry is to bring light and hope to the Jewish people. My friends and I were on our way to a meeting downtown. As I was passing this coffee shop, I sensed in my spirit that God was prompting me to come in and give a message to the person He shows me. When I saw you, I knew in my heart you were the person God wanted me to speak to." Right now, you might be thinking the same thing as I was thinking when I heard this: it sounds too off the wall to be true. How could she have known that I was Jewish, and why was God sending her to me! After her words to me, I looked up at her and gazed at her friends who were standing in the background. It was not what she said that got my attention; I had heard that before at Jews for Jesus. It was the look in her eyes that touched me. She had a look of peace and contentment on her face that was unexplainable. I started to put the pieces together and understand that these experiences I was having were not a coincidence. Even though I didn't comprehend all the implications of what this meant, I knew I wanted to find out. She told me her church, Glad Tidings, was across the street and asked me to go there with her to speak to the head administrator. In spite of my stoned out condition, I found myself saying, "Yes, I will go with you."

When I got to the church, she ushered me into a room where an aged, kind-faced women was sitting and typing. She looked at me with a motherly expression, and said, "My dear why in the world is a beautiful girl like you looking so disheartened and down in the dumps?" I was surprised at her instant assessment of my state of mind. I didn't answer her right away. I was still trying to evaluate the situation, and figure out how she knew my condition without me saying a word. She continued to press the matter. My emotions opened up like a flood gate. I broke down and started to weep uncontrollably. Without any more prompting, I told her that I felt like giving up, I didn't want to live any more. She looked at me very intently, and said firmly but tenderly, "You are not a loser. God has brought you here for a reason. Linda (the woman who confronted me in the coffee shop) and I are going to get you the help that you need." She then proceeded to tell me about a Christian organization named The Walter Hoving Home which is a place where women go to learn about God and make a new start. She explained that they were a Christian based residential free ministry. Their purpose is to help women develop a relationship with God, and discover what plans God has for their lives. Immediately I was skeptical. I thought to myself, "If I couldn't get it together after spending 2 years in treatment at Daytop, why would this place be any better?" I still wasn't convinced that God cared about me and had a plan for my life. Even though I had so many doubts, I wanted desperately to believe there was a God who loved me and would forgive me. She noticed my misgivings, and assured me that she had sent other women to this place that graduated and were doing wonderful things with their lives. I said to myself, "Dawn, what do you have to lose?" I was out of control and

REVELATION—GOD'S CALL

deeply depressed, and knew my options were running out. If I kept going on with the way I was living, the only thing I could expect was to wind up in a mental institution or dead. So, I told her I would go. She called and spoke to the administrator at the Walter Hoving Home. They told her they would be glad to take me, but I had to wait 2 weeks for their next opening. I was so scared. There was a battle raging inside of me. One voice said that it was hopeless and won't work; the other voice said, you've been given another chance to claim your life back. I chose to believe the second voice was the voice of God, who wanted me to take that chance.

2 weeks later, on a cold, snowy December afternoon, Linda and the administrator from Glad Tidings Church drove me upstate to a small town in Garrison, New York, where the Walter Hoving Home was located. As we pulled into the driveway, I was struck by the beauty of the English Tutor mansion covered with snow that resembled a wintery postcard. It sat on 10 acres of property covered with elm trees, weeping willows and a water brook that ran across the property. When I went inside, a group of women were waiting for me. They took me upstairs to the room I was going to be sharing with five other women. All I wanted to do was to get into bed since I was feeling really sick from kicking the drugs. I asked them if they were going to give me any medication to come off the pills. They said the only thing they gave the girls while coming off the drugs was love and lots of prayer. They assured me that although it would be uncomfortable for a couple of weeks, when it was over, I would feel like new. I grunted and wondered why I had agreed to come to this place. It wasn't that I was ungrateful at this wonderful opportunity I'd been given, but rather I was extremely scared that if this didn't work out for me, I would be completely lost forever.

The Christmas holidays came, and the women were busy with all the festivities. They frequently came up to my bedroom to check on me and pray with me. I was sick with leg cramps, insomnia, and a whole host of other symptoms that come along with kicking a drug habit. Even though I was hurting so badly, and spent my days bundled up in bed with 6 blankets to keep warm, I still felt that I was in a good environment. I felt a sense of peace for the first time since leaving Colorado. The staff gave me a Bible and told me to read the gospels. I took their advice and started reading Matthew, Mark, Luke, and John. My first impression of these books was that they all sounded the same. At that point, reading the Bible to me was like reading a book of fairytales. I was still struggling with the idea of being Jewish and believing in Jesus. Again, I heard that voice in my head that said, "Jews don't believe in Jesus." I later learned that Jesus was a Jew, and so was everyone who wrote the Bible, except for Mark and Luke.

Christmas ended and it was the New Year, 1984. I slowly started to crawl out of bed. At this point I was able to come downstairs and have my meals with the other women. After every meal, they had prayer time and a short Bible study. As I started to feel better, which was a very slow process; I paid more attention to what was being discussed during the Bible studies. I saw the excitement and enthusiasm in the other girls which was a great witness to me. They walked around with smiles on their faces, and I noticed their attitude of determination to change their life. As I talked with them I discovered their stories were similar to mine. I was not the only one who had messed up more than once. They talked about abuse in their childhood, struggles with habits that were difficult to conqueror, feelings of being a failure, and other emotions they were battling with. The one common thread they all had in common was expounding on how Jesus had taken their pain, guilt and brokenness and turned them into peace, hope and joy. Yet I was still wondering, "Could God do this for me?" I wanted what they had, but I still had my doubts.

One of the requirements during our year stay at the Walter Hoving Home was to attend the school that was on their premises. It was a large classroom with about 40 seats. They had a curriculum with 5 levels to complete. Each level contained books we had to read, scripture we had to memorize, tapes we had to listen to, reports we had to write, and other materials about faith. I didn't mind going to the classes and doing the work; it was a good distraction from all I was experiencing physically and emotionally. For the first month I was there, I went through the motions, did the schoolwork, and had a job in their business office as a typist, yet I still hadn't gotten to the place where I was doing anything about making a commitment to God.

6

Saying Yes to the Call

December turned into January at the Walter Hoving Home. The snow storms left a beautiful blanket of white that covered the property. I survived the drug withdrawals, and my physical health was improving. My mind was rejuvenated, and I was anxious to discover more about this God that everyone at the ministry was talking about. Then the day came that forever changed my life. There was a tape that one of the women received from her aunt called, "Knowing God." It was circulating amongst the women, and there was quite a buzz about its contents. Since the women were so thrilled about the message in the tape, it piqued my curiosity to find out what all the excitement was about. I waited until everyone left the classroom. I was last in line to hear this coveted speaker. The message spoke about Jesus being the fullness that fills everything in every way with Himself (Ephesians 1:23). It explained that when a person invites Jesus Christ into their life, he comes to live in their heart by His Spirit and takes up residence. Literally speaking, the person becomes the temple of the Living God. It says in I Corinthians 6:19, "Do you not know that your bodies are the temple of the Holy Spirit, who is in you, whom you received from God? You are not your own." He inhabits all that we are, spirit, soul, and body. As I listened intently, something was stirring in my heart. When the tape was over, I jumped up and shouted; "I got it!!" I knew that this was the appointed time when God had entered my life. Even though no one was in the classroom but me, the experience was profound; my whole body felt energized from my head to my toes. It felt like my mind had been opened up and a spiritual light bulb has been turned on. I sensed the presence of God, and for the first time I understood what the people meant about receiving the Spirit of God, the infilling of the Holy Spirit. (John 8:37; I Corinthians 2:12). I felt so exuberant; I had waited so long for this experience, I could hardly contain myself. All at once my mind flooded with new enlightenment. What I had read in the Gospels about Jesus Christ went from head knowledge to a personal experience in my heart. He had become real to me. Instead of someone I have read about, I felt like I had finally met the person of Jesus Christ and he wanted to have a relationship with me. Now, all I wanted to do was spend time getting to know Him. It can be compared to a person falling in love; all they want to do is spend as much time in that person's presence as possible. The only difference is that this is a spiritual experience, not a physical one. This new relationship gave me hope that life now had something special to offer. This was a new chapter in my life—I knew this was not a fantasy or figment of my imagination. The burden of guilt and shame lifted off my shoulders like a two ton weight. Before opening my heart to God, I was consumed by guilt and shame from the years of drug addiction and failure. These destructive emotions robbed me of any ability to heal. I had such hatred in my heart towards my mother that I wasn't able to have any peace.

Hatred and peace in a persons' heart cannot abide together. When God invades a person's spirit, He brings with Him the power to overcome these horrendous feelings. Since He is the prince of peace, He brings that same peace to the person. This was the peace I had been searching for all my life, and now I had it.

When I shared what happened to me with the women they smiled with a nod of approval. Now, the words from the people who had shared their faith with me made sense. I saw them with new eyes. The joy and peace I had seen on the faces of the people who had witnessed to me—from Jews for Jesus, to Linda and the women who came into the coffee shop; and now the woman at the Walter Hoving Home, became a reality to me. I became hungry to read the Word of God whenever I got the chance. I devoured the Scriptures with a new found passion. I wanted to learn all that I could about my new best friend, Jesus. Instead of spending all my time with people, I longed to go down to the Prayer Room in the basement and speak to the Lord. Now that I was in this wonderful relationship with God through His Son Jesus Christ, my entire focus became learning everything I could about my new found faith. The only way to learn about that faith is by talking to God and reading His Word. Now that I've experienced that new enlightenment, I wanted to talk to God, and I wanted Him to talk to me. That is what prayer is all about—talking to God. It's similar to building a relationship with a friend; the only way you can get to know them is by spending time with them. Even before opening my heart to God, I had an inner knowing when something was right or wrong for me. Now, that God had made His home in me by His Spirit, I was learning to discern what He was trying to say to me. When I read the Bible, I asked God to teach me His ways. His ways are revealed in the Word of God, the Bible. It's the same thing with developing an intimate relationship with God. We talk to God, and He speaks to us in our spirit. The only difference with the relationship with God is that He always leads us in the right direction in whatever we're doing. That is not always the case with friends—they might mean well, but they don't have all the answers. Only God knows the beginning and the end of a matter. He has perfect wisdom.

I knew He had touched my life and transformed my heart. The guilt and shame I lived with for all these years was gone. Before, my heart was consumed by condemnation, guilt, and fear, but now God was replacing those feelings with love for me and others. The poet in me likes to put it this way—I felt like I was clean and revived like a sparkling white snowflake on beautiful winter day.

If I can accomplish one thing by sharing my salvation experience with you, it's to show you that no matter what you have done in your life, there is a God who loves you so much and wants desperately for you to allow Him to come into the center of your life and give Him a chance to show you how awesome your life can be with Him at the helm. He's waiting for that opportunity with you.

7

Developing a Relationship with the Lord

It was the end of a long freezing cold winter. The first hint of spring was evident in the budding of the trees and sweet smelling honeysuckles. I was excited about my faith and the beautiful surroundings. On a warmer than usual late spring day, the staff challenged the women to fast and spend time alone with God for the day to see what revelations He would give us. The plan was to get back together in the evening to share our experiences. I went down to the Prayer Room to talk to the Lord. I asked God, "What can I share with the women?" To my surprise, I heard God say, "Get a pen and a piece of paper and I will show you." I was so excited! This was the first time I could hear the Lord speak to me and give me instructions. I scrambled to find something I could write on. Quickly, I tore a piece of paper out of my notebook and started to write. The words spilled out on the paper and I wrote my first poem, "Shine Bright the Light." Let me share it with you.

DEVELOPING A RELATIONSHIP WITH THE LORD

SHINE BRIGHT THE LIGHT

Shine bright the Light
on tortured souls.
Release all the pain and suffering
as only You can do.

Grasp all the hands in unity,
and let us march as true conquerors.

Love and Truth
abandon us no more.
We are Your children.
It is only You we seek for deliverance.

Joy and Peace
are our rewards.
What more can we ask?

We are Your soldiers,
and we will fight to the
death to preserve Your
Honor and Glory!
Zion

Debra Vatulano

After writing it, I was shocked—I had written the poem in 10 minutes. I had never written a poem like this one. Before writing this poem, the only poetry I had ever written was a couple of sentences about love. Now, I couldn't wait to get back with the other women and share the poem the Lord had so graciously given me. I also was curious to see what nuggets of wisdom God had imparted to them. After God gave me that first poem, I started to write whenever I got the chance. Then, one of the women in the business office who was part of the staff heard about my poem "Shine Bright the Light" and decided to make a bookmark out of it. I was so pleased. Now, I could share my poetry with other women who were coming into the ministry. Life with God was as good as it gets, and I was filled with His wonderful joy. I knew I was loved by the Creator of the universe. The difference between mans' love and God's is that God's love is unconditional; He loves us for who we are, His love is not based on our performance. Contrary to what some people think, God is not a mean tyrant sitting up in Heaven waiting to condemn us for every mistake. To me that meant everything. I had spent my life believing that love was based on what I did, not on who I was as a unique individual. In this performance driven society, everything is measured by our performance. It's not that way with God. He loves because it is His nature—God is love.

One hot, balmy, late July day, a woman who had graduated the program came to pay us a visit. We had heard about her, and we all crowded around to hear her extraordinary testimony. She shared with us how God delivered her from mental illness and psychosis. She had been committed to a mental institution due to her episodes with schizophrenia, which caused her to hear voices. At times, because of her violent behavior, they had to put her into a padded cell for days at a time. She said that her family and the staff at the mental institution gave her a negative prognosis; they concluded that she would never get better. She went on to tell us about a woman who was permitted to come to the institution to witness to the patients about God's message of deliverance and freedom in Jesus Christ. When the woman spoke to her and witnessed her behavior, God gave the woman a word of knowledge and she was able to discern that she was possessed by evil spirits. The woman took pity on her, and arranged with the staff to come for regular visits to see her. She spent time sharing the Scriptures with her specifically how Jesus delivered different people from demonic possession (Luke 4:33-38). She told us that she would get angry when the woman spoke about deliverance. Then one day everything changed for her. The woman came as usual, but this day was different. The woman asked her if she could pray with her. She agreed to the prayer. She said when the woman prayed that the demonic spirit would come out of her and leave her alone, she fell to the floor and started to shriek. The woman persisted with the command for the evil spirit to come out of her, and leave her alone. Then she stated that something happened to her that was miraculous. She convulsed on the floor and immediately the evil presence left her. When she got up from the floor she knew that she had been set free. The voices that had tortured her for years were gone. She told the woman who had prayed for her that she had been involved in witchcraft. The woman explained to her that following the occult and the practices of black magic invites demons to take a person captive. The woman asked her if she would like to receive Jesus Christ as her Lord and Savior. She said yes. She said when she asked Jesus Christ to come into her heart and deliver her from the mental illness and the voices she was hearing, she knew she had an encounter with God. The demonic oppression that had tortured her for years was lifted. She told us that after that invitation to invite Christ into her life everything changed. Soon afterward she left the hospital and went to live with her family. She applied to college and was accepted. Four years later, she received a degree in counseling and graduated with honors. After hearing that testimony the women at the Walter Hoving Home were amazed and speechless. I was intrigued by her story. I told her a little about my testimony, and asked her if God will reveal Himself to me in a similar manner. She answered me and said, "He will in His own timing, and in His own way."

That same night after I had asked the woman the question about God revealing Himself to me in a supernatural way I got my answer. I went to bed and fell asleep. Shortly afterwards, I was awakened to a petrifying sight. I saw the outline of a dark, evil presence standing over my bed with hands lifted upward holding what appeared to be a knife. The level of terror I felt was overwhelming. Immediately, I started to pray and cry out to God for His help. What happened next showed me beyond a shadow of a doubt that God is who He says He Is in His Word. As I was praying and calling out for deliverance from this evil thing at my bedside, I felt something happen to me so incredible that it's difficult to describe. I felt a sensation of liquid heat combined with indescribable warmth penetrating through my body. It started at my feet, and traveled up toward my head. It was not only the intense heat that was so amazing, it was the sense of peace and love that shot through my entire being that overwhelmed me and took my breath away. After it traveled throughout my body and reached the top of my head, I fell asleep. The experience lasted less than a minute, yet it shocked me to the core. The next morning, I woke up and realized that God not only answered my request, but He also allowed me to have a taste of His awesome presence. The Bible describes God as a "consuming fire." When he led the children of Israel in the wilderness toward the Promised Land; He followed them in a cloud by day and in a blazing fire by night.

Since I had so much bondage in my life, this was God's way of reaching out to me to show me that He was real, and His love for me was immeasurable. I only had this experience once, but it left a profound impact on my faith even to this day. My reasons for sharing this with you is to let you know that God will do whatever it takes to make Himself known to a person. In my case, when He saw that I was sincere, He responded by giving me a spiritual experience in a physical way. Before opening my heart to Him, this would have been impossible, but now that I was His child by faith, He was willing to award me that precious gift of His tangible presence.

God continued to show me snapshots of how He had been there in the background throughout my life. When I was approaching my teenage years, there was the struggle to find my own identity. Like all young girls, I needed someone I could confide in. The changes I was experiencing physically and emotionally were overwhelming. As I shared with you regarding my childhood, I didn't have anyone in my family who understood me. So, I turned to the God I did not know at the time. Even though I didn't know God personally, I always believed there was a God and that He cared about me. I started a diary, (letters) that I addressed to God, revealing my insecurities and my fears of growing up. When I poured out my heart to Him, there was a sense of comfort and peace that He heard me.

Fast forward to my adult working years, I recall a day when I was late for work in a state of frenzy. I hate being late even to this day. I was rushing through Port Authority Bus Station when I saw two women standing at a large table, selling Bibles. Naturally, at that time I had no interest in purchasing a Bible. As I walked briskly past the table, I felt a prompting inside to go back to the table. I wrestled with these feelings, knowing that I was already late for work, and had no interest in looking at Bibles. Yet, the feeling was so strong that I decided to go back to the table. When I did, the women asked me if I was interested in buying a Bible. To my surprise, without a second thought, I said yes. That night after work, I got home and took out the Bible. I didn't have a clue what I was supposed to read, nor did I understand the words inside. To me, the stories appeared to be fiction. Then, I turned to the Lord's Prayer (Matthew 6:9-13). Again I felt a prompting inside that was telling me to memorize the prayer. I did. Next, I turned to Psalm 23, (The Lord is my Shepherd). I memorized that one too. After that night, from time to time I would wonder what all that was supposed to mean. I still didn't understand at that time that God was trying to get my attention. Looking back, I see that He was there all along, gently calling out to me.

8

Learning the Lessons of Faith

The last six months at the Walter Hoving Home was a time of remarkable growth for me. I was looking forward to graduation and starting my new journey with the Lord. During that time God started a process of inner healing in me that would be the foundation for the rest of my life with Him. He taught me the importance of developing a strong prayer life. In order to get to know the Lord it's necessary to spend time with Him. Like any meaningful relationship we pursue, it requires time and commitment. It's the same principal with developing a relationship with God. It's necessary to make time in our busy schedules to go to Him; expose our hurts; tell Him our concerns so that He can help us to gain the victory in whatever we're struggling with. When people commit their lives to Jesus Christ, they're not only forgiven of their sins, but they receive the Holy Spirit (Acts 5:32). He comes into the center of their lives and brings transformation. As we cooperate with the Holy Spirit by allowing Him to open up the wounds from the past and bring His balm of healing and deliverance, we grow into a beautiful, well watered garden. We become the spiritual flowers

God prunes with His own hands. I learned that this does not happen overnight; it's a process. There were times when I made great strides in my faith, and then there were other times when I made foolish choices and suffered the consequences. When I made those unwise choices, I'd go back to God and ask Him for the wisdom to get back on track. For example, during the first few months at the Walter Hoving Home, while going to school to learn the Bible, we were encouraged to read a certain amount of chapters in a week. Then, we were given a check list to show if we had done the assignment. I hadn't read all the chapters on the list. Since, I didn't want to look lazy or stupid; I lied and checked off that I read the assigned chapters. In the end, I looked stupid for lying because I was asked to elaborate on what I said I had read, and wasn't able to. God, taught me a lesson that honesty is always the best policy. Thankfully, when we make those mistakes, He understands our weaknesses and will help us to improve in whatever area we're struggling in. The wonderful news is that God in His great mercy and grace will do the work of changing us as long as we cooperate with Him. From the onset of my relationship with the Lord, I knew that in order to change my attitudes of selfishness and rebellion I'd have to submit to His leadership. God knew when He called me that I was a mess, yet He still wanted to develop a relationship with me. He understood it would take time and investment to bring about a transformation in me. That's what I love about God; He doesn't ask us to do all the work alone. He's always there to lead, guide and direct whenever we need His help. The greatest miracle for me was that I started to see myself differently from the way I was in the past. The guilt, the fears, the doubts and insecurities were slowly being washed away.

I was also learning the importance of studying God's Word,

the Bible. The Bible is not like any other book; it is God's Word to us personally, His love letter to lead, guide and give direction in every area of life. When I first started reading the Bible, I found it hard to understand. As I continued to read it, God opened up His Word to my heart so that I could understand Him and receive direction. His Word is a mirror. As I looked into the Word, I was learning who God was, who I was, and how to relate to people. Little by little God would show me in His Word the direction I needed for whatever I was struggling with. Whether I was experiencing rejection, guilt, offense, shame, whatever it might be, God had a solution for the problem in His Word. I learned through reading about the lives of the people written about in the Bible, that God never gives up on people even when they make mistakes. God is looking for an open, willing heart. As long as I allowed God to change me, He was always willing to work with me, never condemning me. The Bible has the power to transform our minds (Roman 12:2). I started to build my faith by confessing what the Word said about me instead of constantly speaking about the negative things I was feeling. For example, there were times when my mind would start harping on my past failures. Instead of listening to that garbage, I would start speaking out and saying, "God has forgiven me of my past failures and mistakes. I refuse to believe that poison." I would search the Bible to find scriptures that talk about forgiveness and my new life in Christ. When I found them in the Bible, I would meditate on them, and then confess them. This way, the next time my mind went into negative thinking, I had the necessary ammunition to combat those negative thoughts. It's a scientific fact that we believe more about what we say about ourselves than what anyone says about us. The saying "act as if until you become," is also true with God's Word, I would say what I wanted to see happen in my life, and as time went on, it was coming to pass. I don't want to give the impression that this is a magic formula. If what we confess aligns with God's will, then He will bring it to pass in His timing. God's Word also taught me about who God is. I learned that He is loving, faithful, merciful, kind, understanding, compassionate, and righteous. His Word would encourage me, and at the same time correct me. The great thing was that He would never give me more than I could handle at the time. Since I had lived my life in so much chaos, I found that the Bible gave me direction, and access to standards of truth that I never found anywhere in the world. God's Word is a light unto my feet, and a lamp unto my path (Psalm 119:105).

As you know from reading my story, my adopted father was not there for me in the way I needed him to be. He was distant and preoccupied. That is never the case with God. He is an ever present Heavenly Father who loves to commune with us whenever we need Him. He is never on a time clock wondering when we'll finish. He is always available to listen to what I have to say. I used to be under the impression that God was too busy to care about me and my problems. I learned from reading the Bible that is not the case. Psalm 139 is my favorite Psalm. It talks about the intimacy we can experience with the Lord. He knows everything about us and can't wait to fellowship with us. When I learned that God loved me and wasn't condemning me every time I did something wrong, I knew I'd hit the jackpot. Where on this earth can we go and expect that we'll be loved unconditionally without judgment? His love is unconditional, which meant the world to me. God's love is not based on my performance. He loves me because it is His nature to love. Even when I'm not faithful, God is faithful to me. I know my sins are forgiven, and I have received that unconditional love by faith. When Jesus died at the cross, He took all my brokenness and gave me all His righteousness. Who wouldn't want that? It wasn't enough for me to just know His love intellectually; I've come to know it deep in my heart. Finally, after a lifetime of misery and self-condemnation I found the place where my soul could rest, right in the arms of my Heavenly Father. The great news is that God does not play favorites like people do. This love and forgiveness is available to anyone who wants it, and is willing to accept it.

One of the most important lessons I've learned is the importance of having a grateful heart. I can't say enough about the importance of gratitude. A grateful heart is an open heart and a giving heart. When I realized how much God had done for me by forgiving me, and giving me another chance at life, my response was nothing but thanksgiving. I started to look at the world around me differently. Before, I never stopped to "smell the roses," now I couldn't get enough of nature and all its glory. God was giving me new eyes to see. The world was opening up to me, and I was responding like a little child full of wonder. All we have to do is look at the beauty of the world around us, the flowers, the waterfalls, the animals in all their uniqueness, man in all his complexities, and the response has to be what an incredible Creator God truly is. He provided all the beauty for us to appreciate. In creation I see God, and thank Him for the beautiful world He has created for me to enjoy.

It's so easy to see what's wrong with ourselves and everyone else around us. God was teaching me to look at people differently. I was discovering that if I looked close enough, there is good to be found in everyone. I have my faults and weaknesses like everyone else. I'm human and capable of making mistakes. When someone hurts me or disappoints me I have a choice. I could let go of the offense, or harbor a grudge and suffer the consequences. Gratitude had to become an attitude of choice rather than feelings for me. God was training me to become skilled at seeing people through His lenses of mercy rather than my own narrow perspective. Forgiveness is a gift we give to ourselves. When I don't forgive, it's like I'm drinking poison—it destroys me on the inside. For example, God was dealing with me about forgiving my dad for not being there for me emotionally. He was showing me all the great things my dad had done for me. When I was young I always had food, shelter and clothing. He took me to the doctor when I was sick. He showed up at my high school graduation and encouraged me to go to college. When I was on drugs, it was my father who would come to some of the worst places where I was living and rescue me. God was showing me that my dad did the best he knew how to at the time. When I thought about the things he did do for me instead what he didn't do, I decided to let it go and forgive him. When I made that choice, I felt a new found love for my dad that I didn't have before. That's what forgiveness offers, love instead of bitterness and resentment. You may be thinking, "If I forgive them, I'm letting them off the hook." That's not true. I found that if I don't take revenge, God in His timing will deal with that person in a way I never could. This new mindset required a change in the way I thought about my life, past, present and future. If I didn't change the way I thought, I was destined to return to the same old destructive behavior patterns. When I focus on all the blessings God has placed in my life, instead of harping on what's wrong with me and everyone else, I can move forward to achieve the things I've talked about, and never accomplished. I make a point everyday when I spend time with the Lord to tell Him what I have to be grateful for. After living a life of selfishness, I had to do these things on purpose, and not give into my feelings.

Every day, we can practice this by thinking purposely at least 20 things we have to be grateful for. No matter how terrible our circumstances might be; there are still things we can be thankful for. I first started to put this into practice on a daily basis when I saw a scripture about gratitude in the Bible. It says in 1 Thessalonians 5:18—"Give thanks in all circumstances; for this is the will for you in Christ Jesus." My way of achieving this was journaling. I would record whatever blessings came to mind. For example, on one occasion I wrote, "God, I am grateful for sunshine, I'm grateful for a place to live, I'm grateful for Your wisdom, guidance and direction, I'm grateful that You're helping me to understand Your Word." That's just one example of a list I compromised in one day. When God sees that willingness on our parts to focus on the good things we have to be grateful for, instead of the things we're not happy about, He comes into the center of our circumstances with His mercy to bring a breakthrough. It may sound like something very small, but when practiced, the impact is life changing. I would encourage you to try doing it, and see if it makes a difference in your life.

One of things I was required to do during my stay at the Walter Hoving Home was to attend confrontation groups. Wow! That was really hard for me. After all the years of burying my pain, I didn't know if I had the strength to face the demons and strongholds lurking beneath the surface. Yet, I wanted to break free from the past and all that held me back. I found that the groups were not condemning. They gave me the opportunity to listen to other women share similar life struggles. I came to realize that my grief and anguish was not unique, I was not alone. In this safe environment at my own pace, I was opening up and sharing my feelings. Finally, I was taking the mask off and allowing others to hear my story. Slowly but surely, God was calling me into accountability to confront myself. One of the names of the Holy Spirit is Counselor (John 14:26). He was pointing and putting His finger on the root of my problems instead of letting me just bandage them up on the surface. This had to be one of the most difficult things for me to deal with in my life, confronting the ugliness inside and feeling the brunt of it. When I allowed myself to feel the pain, I was able to grieve and start forgiving myself. The more I was willing to look at the many layers of pain, the more grace and mercy He poured out for me to overcome them. I started to see that my insecurities and fears came from a root of rejection that I developed in childhood from my mother's attacks; physically and verbally. I was overly sensitive. Any time someone did not agree with me, or gave me any type of correction, I would feel offended and walk away. Because of my lack of confidence I couldn't discern the difference between constructive criticism and real offense. That was particularly true when it came to the many jobs I had over the years. If I had conflict for any length of time with a superior, I would feel that I was being treated unjustly and quit. Instead of confronting my feelings in a healthy way, I would assume that I was being picked on, and they didn't like me, or appreciate me. As a result of this attitude, I missed out on so many great opportunities. In the confrontation groups, I was asked the hard questions. For example they would ask, "What hurts you the most? What is it about yourself that you don't like? What was the worst experience you ever had? Do you believe that you are worthy of being loved?" Confronting these questions gave me the chance to expose my real emotions, and it also gave me the chance to see that I wasn't alone—other women struggled with the same things. After every group, the women would hug each other and commit to pray for whatever issues were brought up. After each group, I felt stronger, and noticed that I was starting to heal inside from destructive feelings that plagued me.

One of great blessings I experienced while still at the Walter Hoving Home was a visit from my parents. I had been communicating with them by phone, and now they wanted to see me. The day they came up to visit me, I was very nervous. Because of the unresolved feelings between us, I was apprehensive about how our time together would work out. Even with all my anxieties, when I saw my mother and father come into the room, my heart skipped a beat. In spite of all the brokenness in my childhood, and the wall between us, deep down I still felt love for them. They both looked very pleased to see me. They could see that I looked happier and healthier. I was glowing with God's love and wanted them to notice it. We spent the day going around the beautiful grounds, and my father remarked that "the place looked like the Garden of Eden." Our conversation was light, and they didn't bring up the past. They told me that when I graduated Walter Hoving I could come and stay with them until I figured out what I wanted to do next with my life. The prospect of living with them was scary, but their offer of generosity was very much appreciated. God was putting the pieces together one by one.

Toward the end of my time at the Walter Hoving Home I got baptized. At first I felt a bit conflicted about it since there was still a part of me that believed Jews don't get baptized. Yet, I was embracing all that my relationship with Jesus Christ entailed, and the Bible clearly states that we should be baptized to "fulfill all righteousness" just as Christ did (Matthew 3:13-17). Being baptized for me was a glorious experience. When I came up out of the water, I felt clean (spiritually), knowing that the old person with all the baggage of sin was washed away and I was a new person in Christ. By being baptized, I was making a public testimony of my faith in Jesus Christ.

The last few months before graduation were an exciting time. I was making preparations to go back into society and start a new life. Around that time, I made friends with a woman who came up from New York City to encourage the women and answer any questions we had regarding the challenges of living as a Christian woman in society. We bonded quite nicely and after a short time she asked me if I would be interested in coming to live with her and share the rent. I wasn't sure what to do because as I mentioned, my parents offered me the opportunity to come and stay with them. After some thought, I decided it might be better for me to take her up on the offer. She was attending a large church called Brooklyn Tabernacle and this would give me the opportunity to fellowship with other believers and make new friends. I talked it over with my parents, but they were not convinced this was the best choice for me. They felt I would be better off if I stayed with them. I could live rent free while I worked and saved my money. Nevertheless, they told me that if it didn't work out with this woman I could come and live with them.

Finally after 1 year at the Walter Hoving Home it was graduation day. The staff had prepared all kinds of festivities and ceremonies for the women who were graduating. They made it very special for us. We wore blue caps and white gowns over our dresses. My emotions and anticipation were marked with frenzy and exhilaration. We spent hours beforehand styling our hair, putting on makeup and sharing last words of excitement about finally completing the program. The graduation ceremony was in the chapel which was on the grounds, and it was packed with people eager to see us graduate and take the next step in our journeys. During the ceremony we were each congratulated and handed a certificate stating that we had completed the requirements of the program. I was feeling a great sense of accomplishment. I remembered all the times I felt like giving up. Today was a day of victory, and I cherished every moment of it.

PART III
Transformation/ Living a New Life

9

Starting Over

Starting over for me was like a baby coming out of her mother's womb for the first time and being confronted with a strange new world. It was a time of adjustment. I was feeling a bit like a fish out of water swimming on dry land. For the last year, I had lived out my faith in a protected environment; sheltered and nurtured by the staff and other women. Now, the choices and decisions I made had to be different than the past if I was going to embrace the good things God was planning for me. I had the right ingredients to succeed with Christ living in me by the Holy Spirit, yet the question remained: would I be willing to surrender and do things God's way which would make the difference between success and failure? I'd love to be able to say I did everything correctly without error, but then I wouldn't be telling the truth. Yes, the desire was there, but walking it out can be difficult after years of making bad choices. When a decision is made to follow the Lord, we're instantly enlisted into the armies of the Living God with Jesus Christ as our Commander. As in every war, we have an enemy. In the case of the Christian it is satan the devil. As the Bible says, "he comes only to steal, kill and destroy" (John 10:10a). Before I entered into this spiritual warfare as a believer, I was under the impression that the devil was a character that dressed up in a red suit and carried a pitchfork—a funny little imp who showed up on Halloween. I quickly learned this was not the case. He is a very real enemy who will make every effort by using his demonic evil forces to attack and conquer. Even so, there is no need to be afraid of him because God has total authority over the devil. If a believer will **totally** surrender to God, they have no need to fear the devil. The Lord will come like a mighty warrior and defeat the powers of darkness when we call upon His name.

After graduation from the Walter Hoving Home, I immediately moved in with the friend who invited me to live with her. At first, we got along famously. I was looking for a job and going with her to a great Bible believing church. Everything seemed wonderful. As I had mentioned in the beginning of my story, I suffered from extremely bad cramps the first two days of my monthly cycle. During our first month living together something really awful happened. I got my period and was in very bad pain. I was curled up in bed in a fetal position, suffering dreadfully. My roommate came home from work and stepped into my room. She saw me lying there curled up like a ball. She asked me, "What's the matter with you?" I explained to her about my periods and the pain I went through in the beginning of my cycle. She stared at me with a bizarre expression on her face. What she said next really wounded me. She said to me, "Dawn, are you sure you're not high on something?" I couldn't believe she was asking me this question. I told her, "No, that's the last thing I want to do." I attempted to explain the situation to her again to no avail. She looked at me with disapproval in her eyes and walked out of the room. I couldn't believe this was happening. Without giving me the benefit of

STARTING OVER

the doubt, she was condemning me for something that I didn't do. After she left my room, I could hear her on the phone in the next room speaking to someone at the Walter Hoving Home. She was telling them she suspected I had taken drugs. As a precaution, they called my parents, and told them about her accusations. My parents called me to find out my side of the story. I told my parents the truth about what was happening with me. My father said, "Dawn, I'm coming down to the apartment to speak to you." What a horror this was. I was feeling so confused and hurt that she had caused all this unnecessary chaos. Now that I was being falsely accused, I would have to defend myself. After a couple of hours, my father rang the bell and she let him in. He asked her what was going on. She proceeded to repeat the same false accusations to my dad. After he heard her version of this dreadful tale, he asked me to tell him my side of the story. When I told him the details of what had occurred, he looked at me very intently. I started to cry. What he said next really warmed my heart. He said, "Dawn, stop being upset. Your mother and I are aware of the pain you experience with your monthly cycle. I can see by looking at you that you haven't taken drugs." He turned to my roommate and told her that she had a lot of nerve to have caused all this turmoil for nothing. He went on to say, "My daughter is not on drugs and I'm annoyed that you called the Walter Hoving Home and got everyone there upset." He told me to pack my belongings; he was taking me back home with him. Wow, was I relieved. For the first time in years, my father trusted me. I left her apartment and said goodbye. I had learned enough to know that holding a grudge against her would accomplish nothing. If I didn't let go of the hurt, it would poison my heart and interfere with me developing new friendships. God had taught me an extremely valuable lesson through this horrible incident. I learned that trusting people takes time, it doesn't happen right away. I had only known this woman a very short time. Instead of agreeing to live with her immediately, I should have taken my parents' suggestion and gone to live with them first. Then, after we had been friends for a while, and I knew her character, I could have taken the next step to move in with her. At that time, my personality was still somewhat naïve. I had a tendency to trust people too quickly. One of the unfortunate things about addiction is that it stunts a person's emotional growth. Now, I had to learn to use discretion. It was no longer acceptable for me to make decisions based upon my feelings at the moment—that behavior had caused me terrible consequences.

A week after I moved in with my parents, I went to Manhattan to seek employment. God gave me favor, and I landed an excellent position in a German metals company. My job was to be an administrative assistant in the oil department. The work was demanding and I spent many evenings working overtime. Life at home was amiable, and my parents were making a concerted effort to be supportive. After all the years of turmoil between us in the past, I was starting to see them in a different light. They were delighted to see me working hard and making an effort to change.

While living with my parents, I ventured out once again into the world of dating. Was that ever a bizarre and hilarious experience! I met one eccentric character after another. There was the short, hairy tycoon who owned a newspaper concession at the train station. He was a pilot in his spare time, and owned a Piper Cheroke double engine airplane. I'll never forget the time he gave me quite a thrill by flying over the tallest buildings in Manhattan. After that exhilarating ride, he then turned the plane around, swooped down full speed gliding the plane over the Long Island Sound in circles. My stomach fell right into my feet, but I was having a grand ole' time. Then there was the industrial psychologist that would show up for our dates in baseball uniforms, riding a stretch limousine ready for a night out on the town. He had an obsession with the New York Yankees and the New York Giants. Was he ever a quirky personality! As a laugh, I invited him to my parents' house for lunch. He showed up wearing a black and white striped Yankee uniform with cleats. That meal was quite the experience. My parents couldn't keep a straight face for a moment, and he didn't seem to mind it one bit; in fact, he loved getting the attention. Then there was the executive vice president of the metals department in my company. He wouldn't leave me alone until I agreed to let him walk me from the office to Grand Central Station. After knowing him a couple of hours, he declared his uncontained passion and invited me to go skiing with him for 2 weeks in Switzerland. Thanks to God, I had developed some wisdom by now, and told him, "Thank you, but no." I really didn't know what to make of these men, but overall, I was having fun and experiencing what it was like to enjoy life without drugs.

10

New Opportunities: Growing in Faith

After working for a couple of years I decided I needed a change. After praying and seeking God on the matter, I decided to look into attending Bible College. I called the staff at the Walter Hoving Home and asked them if they could suggest a school for me. They suggested applying to Christ for the Nations in Dallas, Texas. The thought of leaving New York and going completely across the country to a city I wasn't familiar with was intimidating, but after mulling it over, I decided it would be a great opportunity. I spoke to my father about it, and miracle of all miracles, even though he was not a believer in Christ, he not only agreed it was a great idea; he offered to pay for it. He had witnessed the change in me, and was happy to help me with the expenses. Since I had been working and saving money, I told him I would pay for books, food and living expenses. He said he would pay for the tuition and housing. I applied for the fall semester and got accepted. So, in 1987 with two suitcases in tow, I boarded a plane and flew to Dallas. When I got off the

NEW OPPORTUNITIES: GROWING IN FAITH

plane, I caught a cab and headed to the school, where I checked in and was escorted to my living quarters. It was a small apartment on the campus to be shared with four female roommates. When we met, to my delight they all were sweet, down to earth woman who had made significant sacrifices to go Bible School. The apartment was small but cozy. There was a living room, eat-in-kitchen, and two bedrooms. I shared a bedroom with a very conservative southerner who loved to get up in the mornings, get her tea, and sit on her bed quietly praying for God's direction for that day. My other two roommates who occupied the other bedroom were as different as Felix Unger and Jack Klugman from *The Odd Couple*. One of them was a short, funny whimsical gal from Canada; the other was a reserved intellectual from Connecticut. Although we were all very different from each other, the Lord helped us to communicate and work out our differences when they came up.

Classes began and I was fascinated with my courses. For my first semester, I had chosen a wide variety of subjects, such as Old Testament Survey, New Testament Teachings of Christ, World Evangelism, Sign Language, Prayer and its Purposes, and Marriage and Family. Without much difficulty, I immersed myself in my studies and was amazed by all the new discoveries I was making about Christ and the Kingdom of God. God is an endless source of knowledge, and no matter how much I learn about Him, there is always more to explore. One of my favorite things about the school was the international students who came from all over the world. I was being exposed to people and cultures that I had only read about in books. For the first time I made friends with people from places like Nigeria, Philippines, South Africa, Ghana, the Netherlands, Canada and many other places around the globe. The international students were extremely focused, and they displayed tremendous gratitude to have the opportunity to come to America to learn how they could better serve the Lord. God was teaching me that He is not only the God of white Americans, but He is the God of every nation, culture, tongue and tribe. He is the God of anyone and everyone who will invite Him into their heart. We are all His creation, and He longs to have a relationship with us. That is one of the many things I love about the Lord, He doesn't play favorites. When we come into His family by faith, we all become His children, regardless of our backgrounds. We are all equally important to Him. That was so freeing for me to learn that I was loved unconditionally by God just because I was His child. That might not be the case in our natural families, but God is an equal opportunity Father. In our performance driven society, we are often told that success is measured by what we do, not who we are. That is never the case with our Heavenly Father. His love is a well that never runs dry.

Besides the awesome privilege of taking all these fantastic courses, God was also teaching me crucial lessons about faith, and the how to use it practically in everyday life. I was learning that faith is not some pie in the sky ethereal concept where we float around on a halleluiah cloud, but it is very concrete in its essence and application. Faith to me is the process of learning to put absolute trust and confidence in God's power, love and goodness (Colossians 1:4). The Bible also says that without faith it is impossible to please God (Hebrews 11:6a). There were times I still struggled with trust. Due to my lack of confidence in the authority figures who were supposed to be my role models, it was challenging for me to believe in people. But God is nothing like people, He can be trusted, and He is always faithful. As humans we are taught from infancy to rely on our five senses. Faith requires trusting what God says rather than relying on our feelings, and what they dictate. Feelings are fickle. They change constantly, but God's Word is eternal. It never changes. The more I practiced trusting God instead of my feelings, the more I started to grow and mature. Jesus Christ was and is the Master of true faith. During the time He walked on the earth, He did 100% of whatever His Heavenly Father told Him. My desire was, and still is, to sit at the feet of the Master and learn His ways. I started getting up every morning at 6:00, one hour before my first class. When the apartment was silent and my roommates were still sleeping, I would get out of bed, get dressed, make a cup of coffee, go into the living room and kneel down next to the couch. During that early morning hour, I would talk to the Lord. I would tell Him what I was feeling, the struggles I was experiencing, and ask Him for the grace to love people on a daily basis. I would always end my time with Him by expressing my gratitude for everything He was doing in my life.

Yet, in spite of all the ways I was learning and growing, I found myself still struggling with my thoughts. The mind is the battlefield and that is the place where the victory is either won or lost. Before coming to Christ, for 32 years I was programmed to behave according to my fleshly desires. Now that I wanted to live for God, I knew that if I gave into the dictates of my flesh, I would wind up right back where I started from. After years of not having a steady boyfriend, I was struggling with my sexual desires. I had met a man on campus who was also a Jewish believer. We were spending quite a bit of time together and I was growing fond of him. When we were together, there were times when our conversation would take on a sexual tone. He would go into detail about his relationship with a past girlfriend which would cause my mind to have sexual thoughts which were distracting me from my studies. In my younger years in college, I had made the mistake of focusing on men rather than my studies, and I certainly didn't want to make that mistake again. So, I broke the relationship off. I needed to get control of my thought life, and I knew it was time to ask for help. There is something about bringing things into the light that dispels the darkness and brings freedom. It was scary opening up about these very private feelings to my friends. I felt uncomfortable. Yet, some of them were dating, and I thought that they might be having similar struggles. Sharing my thoughts and getting them out in the open was giving me the freedom to conqueror old patterns of destructive thinking. Another way I found success in conquering destructive thoughts was to find verses in the Bible that dealt with the area I was struggling with at the time. God's Word has an answer for all the emotions humans wrestle with… fear, insecurity, doubt, and the list goes on and on. For example when I had doubts about how my future would turn out, I turned to the Bible for encouragement. Even though I was learning to trust God in all things, I still had difficulty taking things one day at a time. I had the tendency to over analyze a matter rather than wait for the Lord's timing to work things out. I had seen Him come through for me time and time again, yet, I would set up obstacles in my mind why I could fail. But, the difference now, was that I had the tools to choose to think differently. Whenever these negative thoughts bombarded my mind, I would wield the sword of the Spirit (Ephesians 6:10-18), God's Word. By confessing the Word out loud, I was engaging in spiritual warfare. In essence I was telling the powers of darkness to get behind me, and leave me alone. This is what Jesus did when the Holy Spirit led Him into the wildness (Matthew 4:1-10). The devil was tempting Him, and the only way He responded to satan

NEW OPPORTUNITIES: GROWING IN FAITH

was by quoting God's Word. It worked for Him, and it was working for me. God's Word is the spiritual armor against the demonic realm.

One of my fondest memories of Bible School was Thanksgiving Day. My friend Paula and I prepared a feast for the international students who couldn't go home for the Holiday. It turned out to be an awesome day. We were given permission by the staff to use one of the unrented apartments for married couples. We had so much fun preparing the yummy delectable's that people enjoy during Thanksgiving. We made turkey with gravy, my mother's recipe for stuffing, mashed potatoes, broccoli with cheese, Caesar salad, and pumpkin pie with whipped cream. There were about 20 of us celebrating together. We ate, fellowshipped, and had a marvelous time while one of the students from South Africa played his guitar. We sang and worshipped God for His goodness. Everyone left feeling loved and part of the great big family of God.

After a year of learning and making some awesome friends, it was time to leave School and go back home to New York.

11

Embarking on Marriage

When I got back to New York, my plans were to live with a close girlfriend I knew before attending Bible College. Shortly after getting settled in her house, I looked for temporary employment as a legal secretary, and applied to become a counselor at one of the U.S. branches of Teen Challenge. Since I had dealt with drug addiction, I wanted to give back to teenagers and young adults who were struggling with drugs, and any other forms of addiction. I contacted Teen Challenge and filled out an application. They contacted me back and told me that they would be glad to have me, but I had to have a car. Unfortunately, I didn't have a car at the time, but my mother had a second car that she was looking to sell. I told my parents about my desire to work at Teen Challenge, and that I would need a car in order to be accepted for the position. The particular branch I was applying to needed someone to live in the facility. They were looking for someone to counsel the women on issues stemming from abuse and addiction. In the interim, I landed a position in a law firm in midtown Manhattan. Shortly afterwards my parents informed me that they had already sold the car. Needless to say, I was disappointed. Since I had just finished Bible School, I didn't have the money to buy a car. My only option at the time was to work and save the money to buy one. As it turned out, a month later the position was filled at Teen Challenge. Even though my plans were temporarily thwarted, I wasn't going to give up. I believed in God's timing. When the time came, I would have the opportunity to serve him as a drug counselor or in any other capacity that He opened the door for me. It didn't matter where the opportunity came from, what really mattered was to have the chance to help people work through the same issues that I had struggled with. My desire has always been to encourage people with the truth. The Bible says: "You shall know the truth, and the truth shall set you free." (John 8:32). I know how painful it is to face the truth about ourselves, but until we are willing to walk in our truth, we can never expect to be free and live the life God destined for us to have.

One snowy winter afternoon, I was browsing in a newspaper/coffee shop during my lunch hour. As I was flipping through one of the latest fashion magazines, I noticed from the corner of my eye a tall, rather husky guy looking at me smiling. My first thought was to put the magazine down and run out of the shop. But before I could make another move, there he was, in my face, introducing himself to me. Even though I was hesitant about the encounter, there was something in his big brown eyes that made me feel at ease. He said to me, "Hi, my name is Bobby. I was watching you while flipping through my wrestling magazine—you intrigued me, and I wanted to talk to you." Even though I knew it was a pick up line, I was impressed with his honesty. He asked me if I lived in the area. That seemed like an innocent question, so, I told him I worked in the area. We engaged in some small talk for awhile, and then

I told him I had to get back to the office. He asked me for my phone number. I thought to myself, he's cute and appears to be a nice guy so why not? I gave him my office number, went back to work and didn't think much about it. About a week later, he called and asked me if I would meet him for lunch. I told him I was really busy and didn't have time to talk. I suggested he call me again in another week. My attitude was, "I just got home from Bible school; do I really want to start dating again?" He was really persistent; and I finally agreed to have lunch with him. He took me to a quaint little Spanish restaurant where the seats were snug and intimate. We ate a delicious lunch and he kept the conversation light and unthreatening. He told me that he had never been married before, and he lived with his mother since she was recovering from breast cancer which now was in remission. I dug a little deeper about their relationship, and found out that she had been in a concentration camp during Hitler's reign. Being a Jew, I was intrigued by this bit of information since I had been told from the time I was young about the horrific events the Jews endured in the death camps. After eating, we took a long stroll back to my office. He asked me if he could call me again and I said yes. There was something very kind and genuine about this tall, handsome fellow, and I wanted to learn more about him. He called me again two weeks later and asked if I wanted to get together on a Saturday afternoon. I agreed to meet him. Naturally, after the pain I endured from my breakup with my boyfriend Chris years before, I was cautious about men. From my past behavior, I knew that I had a tendency to get involved emotionally while throwing all prudence to the wind. We met that following Saturday, and to my relief he showed up with a friend. We spent the day walking around Manhattan, laughing and getting to know one another. Later on his friend left and we had lunch. I told him a little about myself, he shared more about himself, and he went into more detail about his mother. From what he told me, she was a remarkable woman. She had endured tremendous pain and suffering in her life, and yet she had a strength and determination to live life with gusto. From what he told me about her, I wanted to meet this woman and hear more about her story. I didn't know where my friendship with Bobby would go, but I wanted to have the opportunity to meet his mother. My life had not been filled with many female role models, and I coveted the chance to get to know this woman that he raved about so extravagantly. I shared my sentiments about it with him and asked if I could meet her. He said that he would talk to her about me and give me a call if she agreed to meet with me. The following week he called me at work. He said he had talked to his mother about me and she not only agreed to meet with me, but she also invited me to lunch at her house. He told me that in the past he was very hesitant to bring any girl home since his mother had such high standards.

That next Saturday, I spent the morning combing through my closet to pick out an appropriate outfit that would fit the occasion. I left my house and took the ferry to Staten Island.

Bobby met me at the Ferry and we took a cab to his house. When I entered the apartment, I was immediately impressed with the impeccably immaculate surroundings. The furnishings were simple yet elegant. Margaret walked into the room and greeted me with a warm, inviting smile. I could see from her tall but emaciated frame that she had been battling an illness that that made her look gaunt; nevertheless, she carried herself with dignity and strength. As soon as I greeted her, she made me feel at ease in her presence. She told me to sit down and offered me a drink. Without further ado, she inquired about how I met her son, asking me directly, "What is your interest in him?" She was like a mother bear protecting her cub. I was a little taken back by her straightforward approach, yet I admired her candor. I understood where she was coming from; he was the only one left at home since his sister got married. At that point I really didn't know where this relationship was going, so I answered her in a non committal, off handed way. I didn't want to admit to her that I was more intrigued with her life story than I was with her son. It was so inspiring for me to be in the presence of someone who had survived such insurmountable abuse and torture. I knew that she could teach me valuable lessons about being an overcomer. Yet, in spite of all her emotional strength, it was the pain in the back of her eyes that drew me to her. I wanted to take her in my arms and hold her close to me. Those were the same feelings I would get about my mother from time to time, but she never gave me that chance.

The three of us ate a simple but tasty lunch while we shared stories of our childhoods and what our everyday lives were like in the present. We laughed and reminisced the rest of the afternoon. After having some coffee and desert, it was time for me to leave. I thanked Margaret enormously for her time and told her what a privilege it was to meet her. She expressed the same sentiments and told me she would like to do it again. Bobby took me back to the Ferry and thanked me for such a wonderful day. He told me he would like to get to know me better, and asked me if I felt the same way. I told him yes. On the one hand, I wanted very much to have a chance at love again, yet on the other hand, the thought of commitment scared me. Since I gave my heart to God I had discovered that healing is a lifelong process. Through this spiritual journey, God had uncovered many areas of brokenness within me that were very painful to process. While growing up I was forced to suppress so many damaging emotions that now the thought of opening up my heart in a love relationship frightened me to the core. A girl's first male relationship is with her father, and when that is impaired, it becomes hard to trust men. My biological father walked out on me and my mother when I was an infant, and my adopted father never protected me from the abuse I suffered by my mother. Even though I had these issues with trust, I didn't want to stay stuck in my past hurts and wounds. God had opened the doorway in my heart for healing, and that included dealing with all relationships. In the Bible, Isaiah 61 is a chapter I love and lean on whenever I need encouragement. It states, "I came to heal the broken hearted and bind up their wounds…to proclaim liberty to those who are held captive…to bestow on them a crown of beauty instead of ashes…the oil of joy instead of mourning…a garment of praise instead of a spirit of despair…instead of your former shame you will receive a double portion…instead of disgrace you will rejoice in your inheritance…and you will inherit a double portion in your land, and everlasting joy will be yours." Those were promises from God, so I knew that He had great things for me, even in relationships.

A few days later, Bobby called me raving about the wonderful time he had when I came to his house to have lunch with him and his mother. He told me that I had made a first-class impression on his mother. I was so pleased to know that she enjoyed my company, and we had made a connection. He asked me to meet him the following weekend, and this time I happily agreed. When we met, we talked about our dreams and goals for the future. He told me how much he enjoyed spending time with me, and wanted to know how I felt about him. I was honest with him and explained about my past challenges with relationships. He listened intently and showed great compassion when I told him about the abuse I endured while growing up. I told him it was important to me if we were going to take the relationship any further, that he never interferes with my relationship with God. I still believed that God wanted to use me to bring a message of healing to hurting people who had been ravaged by abuse. Who better to bring the message of God's redemptive power of deliverance than someone who has experienced it personally? After our conversation, I felt a sense of relief, and knew that he was a man of compassion and understanding.

From that time on, Bobby and I were together whenever I wasn't working. Since he grew up with an Italian father and a Jewish mother, he was exposed to different beliefs. When I shared the Gospel with him, he was very interested, and admitted he had never knew heard such a wonderful message of hope before. He expressed his desire to get to know more about the love and forgiveness of God. He agreed to go to church with me and study the Bible. His willingness to learn about God was a vital component if we were going to go further with our relationship. Since Jesus Christ was the most important Person in my life, I had to have a partner who would be willing to respect my faith.

A year later we got married. Since his mother's cancer came back and she was often ill, we had a very simple ceremony. We moved in the apartment upstairs, in the two-family house that Margaret and her family had rented for 15 years. Bobby and I settled into a life that consisted of work, spending time deepening our relationship, and taking care of his mother Margaret. I enjoyed the time the three of us spent sitting around laughing and sharing stories of good times we had experienced together. Margaret and I had developed a very close relationship. She became the mother that I never had. She was strict with

Bobby and me... but at the same time caring, loving and always willing to do anything she could to help us. It would crush me to see her come home from her appointments after getting chemotherapy. She would run into the bathroom and vomit till she could no longer stand up. It was torture watching this strong, determined woman suffer from the agony of cancer. Many of the early years of my marriage to Bobby focused on attending to Margaret's needs. For me, this was a privilege. Since Bobby and I were working, she got her meals from a government agency for the sick and aged, Meals On Wheels. She hated the food. At night when I came home from work, I would whip up blueberry blintzes, one of my favorites from my mother's recipes. Her eyes would sparkle and she would rave about how much she loved them, and how grateful she was that I thought of her. Still to this day, I marvel at the incredible attitude that she showed. Even though she was suffering, she hardly ever complained. Her only concern was to see her family happy and healthy.

A year later, she lost her battle with cancer and died in Bayley Seton Hospital in Staten Island. At the end, cancer had ravaged her body to the point where she was only 99 pounds. Even in her final days, her message to us was to trust God, stay strong in adversity, love the people in your life, and forgive.

12

Margaret's Story of Survival
In the Concentration Camp in Dachau, Germany

As I've stated from my last account of Margaret Gandini; she was a woman of incredible strength of character. She was the example of a true overcomer in every sense of the word. She survived not only tremendous loss in her family, but she also survived to make it out of one of the worst concentration camps in Germany. Her example of bravery has impacted my life in such a profound way that I want to tell her story of coming 'Out of the Darkness into the Light.' While she was still alive, she shared with me her story of survival from the horrific events of the time she spent in Dachau Concentration Camp. It is a gruesome story, but it is the truth. In honor of her memory, I believe it should be told. Here is her personal account:

I was born in Tachau, Czechoslovakia, on July 1, 1920. I was raised Jewish, but my father would send me on Sunday mornings to the Catholic Church to listen to the gospel.

MARGARET'S STORY OF SURVIVAL

I attended grammar school and high school in Praha on the outskirts of Tachau. My favorite subject was physical education.

I was the only child out of seven to attend college. In 1936 I entered college in Praha University. I was enrolled for one year to become a teacher. Later on, I had a change of heart and transferred to a college for women athletes in Augssig, Czechoslovaka to become a physical education instructor.

In 1939 I graduated and took my first job as a physical education teacher in a school for boys. I taught there for 6 years.

In 1945 World War II was going on, and I was taken by force from school by German SS soldiers because I was a Jew. I was placed in a concentration camp in Dachau, Germany, at the age of 25.

When I entered the camp I was met by thirty SS soldiers who treated me as if I was a traitor to the German armed forces. I was stripped of all my clothes and beaten with a rubber hose until my body was full of blood. Then they made me bring back the buckets of water mixed with salt, which they poured over my entire body.

In my barracks I heard no noise except screams. The uniform they gave me to wear was black and white, but I couldn't put it on due to all the injuries that had been inflicted upon me earlier. The barracks I was in had forty-five other women ranging in age from twenty-five to seventy. I was put on a cement floor in the corner like an animal. The other inmates looked at me with sorrow because they weren't allowed to help me. Four hours after the first attack, six German soldiers came in to see the "new Jew." I was given a new name, 19635. Still to this day I have nightmares remembering the hours I was raped by the six soldiers. Two of them were holding me, while two were raping me from the back, and the other two in the front at the same time. Again, the job was done to the number 19635.

I was then pushed without clothes into the barracks with the other inmates.

After two days in Dachau, it felt like I had been there a lifetime. The next day was a day with more horrors. Again, they called 19635 over the microphone. The door swung open… two SS soldiers picked me up and dragged me, since walking was impossible, to the Butcher room. The big white walls had blood splattered all over them. In that room, I lost seven of my teeth by the hands of an SS soldier. With my blood, I had to write on the walls, "Hitler is a good man." For nine months, they made me carry my teeth around by my neck.

By this time, they believed I would die, but I was strong and stubborn and wouldn't give up. Every hour on the hour the German soldiers would check to see if I was still alive.

The third day was like a holiday! I was able to wear the uniform they gave me when I first arrived. I was given a bed to sleep in. The bed was made of straw, and I had to share it with another inmate. This was the first day there was no beatings, and no questions asked.

The SS guards changed shifts, so a new crew took over who didn't see the new Jew numbered 19635. I was still swollen faced with dried blood all over my body. I was hardly able to walk. That's when they called me in for a demonstration in physical education.

I thought it was too good to be true, but soon found out how misleading it could be when I found myself entering the Butcher room. Strongly I fought; yet, I was stripped of my clothes, and commanded to do fifty knee bends as they pushed me against the wall. The worst mistake I made was to fight back. The punishment was coming and I knew it. It was hard to believe, but they took two bathroom plungers with suctions on the front, and put them on my breasts. They laughed and sang as they pulled on them. Today, the marks are still there.

I was sent back to the barracks, and for punishment for hitting an SS officer I couldn't have any meals for three days. Talking about meals, the menu was: 1) 1 bowl of soup; 2) 6 potatoes and soup at dinner time; 3) 3 potatoes and a glass of milk, only on holidays.

A couple of days went by and they were quiet ones. I never weakened. The hate inside stirred up in me an iron clad will to live. For me to write everything that I suffered and saw others suffer, would take an entire book to describe the dreadfulness and torture that the SS soldiers inflicted on innocent people.

For nine months I wondered WHY? Why were women, men and children being slaughtered, buried alive, and fried just because they were of a different religion?

Day in, and day out, there was no fresh air. We counted the days on the walls…we asked, when will it end? The news came like a time bomb to the camps that the Americans have arrived! Everybody started to run outside to get the air and sun that we hadn't experienced in such a long time. I, like everybody else, ran too, but I fell to the ground; I weighed only ninety pounds.

Everyone was free, and when I woke up I was in a straitjacket in a field army hospital. There I met my friend, Master Sergeant John Gandini.

Although I was free, the hate was still imbedded inside because of the constant visions of the SS soldiers in uniform.

Within four months I was feeling a lot better, and with the help of the Red Cross and my new friend Master Sergeant John Gandini, I found my parents in Germany; they had thought I was dead. The reunion was great, but the hate was still there.

In 1947 at 27 years old, I married my hero, John Gandini, under German law. I had a son I named Robert who was born in December of 1948, and in 1953 I entered the United States of America as a citizen of NO LAND. I had a German passport, yet when the Nazis came, I was thrown out of Czechoslovakia. In 1954 I became an American citizen in Norfolk, Virginia. I will always remember the insanity of the death camp, and feel that Americans should thank God every day for their freedom.

In these years, I traveled with my husband to Spain, Italy, France and Belgium. In 1955, I had a daughter. I like to say that she was made in France, but born in Germany.

In 1963 my husband John passed away from a heart attack, at the age of 52 after completing twenty-four years in the United States Army.

Since that time, it was with the help of good friends and family that I was able to recover from the tragedy. Yet, I still can't forget the years behind the stone walls where nobody could give me an answer to the simple question of WHY??? Why the war, why the concentration camps?

Today, I am employed by the Army Air force exchange service as a Branch Retail Manager. My life and marriage with my husband was beautiful. Yet, I am still tormented by nightmares that conjure up those stored memories. I'll never forget Europe in its worst and most tragic days...

In spite of all the torture and abuse Margaret suffered, she never blamed God, or gave up her faith in Him. There was an anonymous poem written on the walls of the concentration camp. I believe it's pertinent to how Margaret felt.

> "I believe in the sun even when it's not shining;
> I believe in love even when I don't feel it;
> I believe in God even when He is silent."

My motive in sharing Margaret's story with you is not to

bring attention to the atrocities perpetrated on the innocent during Hitler's reign, but to bring attention to a person who triumphed over incredible evil. She had every reason to hate God and stay bitter, but she overcame evil by believing in good. She exemplifies the woman described in Proverbs 31. V. 17 "She girds herself with strength, [spiritual, mental, and physical fitness for her God-given task] and makes her arms strong and firm. V. 25a Strength and dignity are her clothing and her position is strong and secure. 26. She opens her mouth with skillful and godly Wisdom, and in her tongue is the law of kindness—giving counsel and instruction."

Since Margaret never had the opportunity to share her story with the world, I stand up in her place, and let everyone know that no matter what abuse, tragedy or evil has been done to you, there is a God who sees all, and will bring justice to all. She used to say, and I second that emotion, that, "I hated what was done to me, but as a result of it, I have become a stronger,kinder, and more resilient person. I understand what it is to hurt, and my arms are open wide to comfort those who by no fault of their own, had to endure the suffering at the hands of depraved individuals."

Your story of abuse might not have been as catastrophic as Margaret's, but to all who have suffered, the emotions are still the same. We cry, we vent, and even wonder at times, will the feelings ever go away. There is a saying, "time heals all wounds." I don't believe that is necessarily the truth. What I can say from my own experience is that God in time will heal all wounds if we are willing to surrender them to Him. It is a process that requires our willingness to face the root of the pain; then decide how we choose to react to it. If we decide to forgive; allow God to help us come to terms with it, then we can look forward to getting better, and in turn, help someone else get better. The best revenge for all exploitation is not to get back at the perpetrator, but choose to forgive. That is the greatest gift to oneself and others… forgiveness. Even though we might shout, "You don't know what they did to me," whatever it is we can forgive. I know this way of thinking is contrary to our sensibilities, but it will work. Is it hard? Yes, it's very hard. If we don't let it go, what is our options? If Margaret, who was brutally beaten and raped could forgive, why can't we? Let us be our own best friend by choosing to rise above the pain, lay it down, ask God to help us to overcome the feelings, and move on to take hold of all that God has in store for us.

13

Love and Loss

After my mother-in-law died, Bobby and I sank into a depression. Intellectually, we knew that she had suffered and was in a much better place, but we didn't want to go on without her. She had become a bright light to me, and a source of such great strength that without her, I knew life would not be the same. Bobby was depressed, but he didn't react like me. His mother had told him, "Bobby, when I go, I am confident that Dawn will be there for you, and you can depend on her." For me, it was different. It felt like I was losing a mother for a second time. Even though my mother was still alive, we were not speaking. When I married Bobby, my parents did not approve of my choice. They felt I could have done much better, and that he was not good enough for me. They even went as far as to tell me, "Dawn if you marry him, we will have nothing more to say to you." I took it literally. I stopped calling them, and they didn't call me. I felt abandoned by them once again. At a time when I needed them, they were not there for me. When I called them and told them that Margaret had passed away, they offered their condolences, but that was it;

there were no further calls or communications from them. Their rejection hurt me terribly. In the mist of all the loneliness, and feelings of abandonment, the most important thing I did know was that God would never reject me. During this time of sorrow, His gentle hand constantly soothed my broken heart. Whenever I cried out to Him, He was always there to comfort me; He gave me the strength I needed to push on. Strangely enough, it was a time of tremendous creativity for me. What I couldn't express in words, I was able to express in poetry. There were many days and nights when I shut myself up in a room alone with nothing but a pen and paper as my companions. I poured out my heart to God, and wrote, and wrote some more. I kept a journal to make sense of my feelings. This is something I suggest to everyone who has had to deal with loss, rejection, and hurt of any kind. Keeping a journal is a fantastic way to express feelings that are hard to express verbally.

After a couple of very difficult months, Bobby and I talked in depth about our loss, and decided Margaret would have wanted us to go on and keep her memory alive by living the best life we could. Instead of letting this loss tear us apart, we bonded together and developed an even stronger friendship. We were very open and honest with each other about what we felt, and knew it was time to get on with the business of living. We were realistic about what it takes to have a successful relationship. After all my failures in the past in the area of relationships with men, I came to the conclusion that love is not just a feeling, it is an action word. Very often, we romanticize love, and it becomes a fantasy instead of an everyday reality. We look to someone else to meet all our needs, and hold them responsible for our own happiness. I realized that the only one who could meet all my needs was my Heavenly

Father. He is the only One who has that endless source of love that never runs dry. It's unfair to expect people to give us what they might not have to give. That's why so many people in our culture today get divorced. I've heard it said over and over again, "Life is too short to be tied to someone who doesn't make me happy." I don't want to sound old fashioned, but whatever happened to keeping the marriage vows, "for better or for worse, in richer and in poorer, in sickness and in health to death do us part?" Love is a choice, and more importantly, a commitment. There were many days when I didn't feel loving, or didn't feel like being married, but I knew if I listened to those deceitful emotions, I would be alone. My emotions are fickle. One moment they tell me, sit on the couch, eat potato chips, and let Bobby do all the work; the next minute they tell me, that's not fair, you should get up and help him. In Jeremiah 17:19 it says, "The heart is more deceitful than all else, and desperately wicked; who can understand it?" This is a perfect description of living according to our feelings. That's why I find my truth in the Word of God. God respects my feelings, but does not want me to make decisions based upon them alone.

The Bible has a lot to say about marriage and relationships. God instituted the first marriage in the Garden of Eden. In Genesis 2:24 He said, "Therefore a man shall leave his father and mother and shall become united and cleave to his wife, and they shall become one flesh." The Hebrew word for cleave is to stick to like glue. Bobby and I had many challenges and difficult times where we disagreed, but in the end, we both learned how to compromise. For example, Bobby had a tendency to make plans with his friends and not tell me about it. There were nights when it was after 12:00 and I hadn't heard from him. I'd be standing at the window, panicking and wondering where he was. Then, he would walk in, with a big smile on his face as if nothing happened, and say, "Dawn, why are you still up, you should have gone to bed." That would infuriate me. I'd try to explain to him why it bothered me, and he'd tell me, "Dawn, you're overreacting." On nights like that, I chose to sleep on the couch. The next morning, we'd wake up, he'd give me a kiss and apologize and things would go back to normal. He wasn't the only culprit. I had a tendency to be too controlling. When there was a deadline for bills, my first response was to pay it immediately and get it out of the way. He would find nothing wrong with waiting to the last minute. That would get me upset because I would worry that if we don't send it out early and it gets lost in the mail, they will charge us late fees. All this is petty stuff in the bigger scheme of things, but people get divorced over the little things if they are not negotiated. In the end, Bobby and I always found a way to reach an agreement. For us, divorce was not an option.

 Overall, my life with Bobby was rewarding. His comical, easy going personality made the difficult times easier to bear. He was always there to lend a helping hand. His unselfish attitude taught me a thing or two about what it means to be a generous person. I recall one particular incident where he relinquished his will to make me happy. I told him I wanted to get a cat. I had grown up with pets, and knew the joy they bring to life. He had always had a dog, and didn't particularly like cats. After some debate, he agreed to go with me to North Shore Animal League to check out the kittens. After driving for 3 hours and getting lost numerous times, we arrived there in one piece. I jumped out of the car and rushed into the main room. It was a weekend, so they were busy. They escorted us into the area where they kept the puppies and kittens. I was pacing back and forth, like a kid in a candy store desperate for a sugar fix. I wasn't really sure what kind of a kitten I wanted. Then I saw her. She sat in the back of her cage, her oval shaped amber eyes glaring out at me. I was hooked and mesmerized by her presence. I put my hand in the cage (which they tell you not to do), and she lunged her tiny body full force into the bars. She was beautiful, but wild and undomesticated; kind of like me in my earlier years. Even though she was tiny, she was a real spitfire. She looked like a ball of grey fur, with a patch of white under her chin, and white paws with long uncut claws. Bobby looked at me, and said, "Dawn, forget it, this one is too crazy to even consider." I knew that, but wanted her nevertheless. At his advice, I walked away, but still couldn't get her out of my mind. I looked at the other kittens on display, but didn't feel the same connection as I felt with that grey ball of wonder. Then I noticed an older couple looking into her cage, and asking one of the workers questions about her. I lingered in the background trying to determine if they were really interested in her. I heard them discussing it between themselves as to whether or not they wanted to adopt her. That's when I made my move. I ran over to the cage, looked at the couple, and said, "Please, don't take her, I have to have her." They looked at me with expressions of bewilderment. Without words, I could hear them say, "Where did this chick come from?" I stood my ground and told them how much I had fallen in love with her, and couldn't be happy with any other cat. To my amazement, they saw my desperation, and told me, "She's all yours." Meanwhile, Bobby was watching the whole encounter with an exasperated expression on his face. I ran over to him, jumping up and down like a five year old grinning with enthusiasm. At that point, he saw it was a lost cause. He told me, "Okay Dawn, we can get her, but if she turns out to be a handful, you're responsible to take care of her." I agreed, we filled out the necessary paperwork to adopt her, and she became a new addition to our family.

As soon as we left North Shore, we looked for a pet store. They had put her in a box, and I knew that would never work out while I was driving. She was desperate to get out of the box, crying and scratching. We found a pet store a few blocks away. We bought a small cage, clippers to cut her claws, and some other items we needed to get her started at home. Before leaving the pet store parking area, I got in the backseat where I had placed her box, leaned in and picked her up. She started squirming, and scratching me furiously. Bobby got the towel we had brought from home, looked in the trunk and found some gloves. As gently as he could, he grabbed her and held her down. By the way she was carrying on, you'd think we were trying to kill her. I quickly got the clippers and started to trim her claws. I did the best job I could, placed her in her new cage and drove home. After a couple of weeks she calmed down, bonded with me, and even Bobby started to fall in love with her. I named her Sadie—my little Jewish lady. This was an example of one of many incidents where Bobby demonstrated his love and unselfishness. If the tables were turned, I don't know if I would have been as accommodating.

For the first eight years of our marriage, Bobby was an active, healthy guy. He walked two miles a day, and ate healthy food. Due to an issue with alcohol in his younger years, he had developed problems with his liver; his stomach would become enlarged with water, and when it got out of hand, he would have to be admitted to the hospital till the condition was stabilized. Then, the day came that forever changed my life as I knew it. Bobby came home after his usual walk looking very grey and gaunt. I knew immediately something was wrong. I asked if he was feeling alright. He said, "Dawn, I feel weak. I don't have the energy or the strength I usually have during my morning walks." I also noticed that his stomach looked enlarged. I had to take care of a few errands, so I told him to lie down and rest till I got back. When I came back, he was doubled over in pain. He was lying in a fetal position and his face was beet red. Without another thought, I said, "Let's go over to Bayley Seton Hospital." I hated to go to that hospital since his mother Margaret died there, but it was in the neighborhood, and he was in too much pain to travel anywhere else. When we got to the emergency room; they took one look at him and told us that he had to be admitted. They escorted him on a stretcher to a large, stark white room where there was already another patient in bed. I wanted to be supportive, but my heart was in my stomach…I was really scared. They immediately hooked him up with an IV to dispense the medicine to drain the water that had built up in his stomach. That night, after begging the nurses for permission, I stayed with him all night. Even though he was hooked up to an IV and in the hospital, we spent the night laughing and making up funny little songs and silly jokes.

 The next morning I went home to feed the cats, (we had 3 by this time) and clean up. I didn't know what to make of the whole thing. I was frightened because I knew that his condition could be serious. I couldn't imagine my life without him; we were close and I really cared for him. We were married 8 years, and he was only 48 years old. I didn't want to be widow at 44.

 As the week progressed, he was starting to feel better. The doctors had given him enough medication to drain the water from his stomach. He was eating well, and he was no longer in pain. They were planning on releasing him that day. I woke up early and rushed to the hospital to pick him up and bring him home. When I got there, he was no longer in his room. I ran to the nurses' station and asked them where he was. They told me that he had thrown up blood earlier in the morning, and they made a decision to put him in the intensive care unit.

I felt devastated, overwhelmed, and petrified. Besides a few church friends, I was all alone and had no one to turn to. I hadn't heard from my family in years, and that made me feel even more isolated. How was I going to deal with this? I asked the nurses if I could go visit him. They said yes, but told me that he was sedated.

When I walked into the room, I could feel the goose bumps running up and down my body. I felt cold all over, and dizzy. It was a large room, and he was lying in bed between two screen partitions. He was hooked up to all kinds of machines, and they had taken off his pajamas and put him in a white gown. He was out cold; he didn't even know I was there. I sat down and started to pray. "Father, I am scared and feeling so alone, please touch Bobby and bring him back to health; give me the courage to walk through this dark valley no matter what the outcome." I felt sick to my stomach and couldn't control the tears that were flowing out of me like a waterfall. The nurses came in and told me to go home and get some rest. They took my phone number and told me they would call if they had any news. I went home, fell on the couch exhausted from the stress, and screamed out, "This is too much for me to take in, what now?" The old temptations to get pills to dull the pain came rushing in like a broken dam. My throat felt tight; I was having trouble breathing. As much as I hated to do it, I searched the kitchen to see if there were any pills left over from the days when Margaret was still alive dealing with her last bout of cancer.

I found an antidepressant called Wellbutrin. Quickly, before I could talk myself out it, I swallowed two pills. Almost immediately, they took effect. They were so strong that they made me feel like I was spinning in circles, even though I sitting down. I got up to get some water, and I fell on the floor. I was so frustrated and angry at myself that I started to scream, "Why is this happening to me, God I need your help, or I'm not going to make it through this valley." I lay there on the couch engulfed in confusion; I was so exhausted from the emotional pain, I fell asleep. I woke up the next morning fully dressed, and still in the same position from the night before. I still felt a bit dizzy from the pills I had taken. It was another learning experience for me. I saw that taking drugs to deal with trauma only makes the trauma more intense. Instead of the medication calming me down, they made me sick and miserable. I knew that God has delivered me from using pills to medicate the pain. Right then and there, I made a decision that with the Lord's help, I would not go down that road again.

I made a cup of coffee, and looked out the window. It was snowing outside pretty hard, and the room was freezing. My three little cats could sense something was bothering me, and they came one by one and brushed their tails against my leg. I loved those three "whippersnappers" so much, and their presence was a comfort to me.

I hadn't heard from the hospital; so I figured "no news is good news." I decided to call the pastor from the church I was attending; I sure could use his prayers, and any encouragement he had to offer. He told me he was going to bring some elders from the church, and he would meet me at the hospital. When I arrived, and saw Bobby lying there; the same cold feeling went up and down my spine. I didn't want to assume the worst, but from looking at him, the situation appeared bleak. He was lying there in the same condition that I left him the night before; body very straight, with his arms folded across his chest. It was heart wrenching to see him like that. I was used to the big, strong man who always was there to make me laugh. The only thing that gave me some comfort was the expression on his face; his eyes were closed, but he looked at peace.

The pastor and the elders from the church circled around his bed, held hands, and started to pray. Although there was no immediate change in his state, the prayers consoled me; I knew that no matter what happened, God's grace would help me to make it through. After they were done praying, we talked for awhile, and they left. I sat down at his bedside, and started to call his name. "Bobby, if you can hear me; please open your eyes." He never said a word. I stayed for another couple of hours, and decided to go home. On my way out, I spoke to the nurses and asked them what was happening, and how they planned to treat him. They told me that his liver had blown up again, and they planned on taking him to surgery the next morning to put in a stint to block the poisons from further damage. I couldn't believe what I was hearing. Just one week ago, he was walking two miles a day. Now, he was in the intensive care unit fighting for his life. I walked back home feeling shell shocked. I didn't know what would happen…that had to be the hardest part, the unknown. I was plagued with feelings of loneliness. Bobby was my only confidant; whom did I have to turn to now? As soon as I got into the house, I slumped down on the futon chair, closed my eyes and drifted off to sleep. I awoke in the middle of the night; the feelings of abandonment closed in on me; I felt so frightened. I got up and wrote this poem:

SILENT LOVE

In the midnight hour, I awaken to find myself alone.
I am groggy and detached.
My thoughts of fear and desperation surround me like iron shackles.
Oh, how desperate I am for comfort and warmth.
I look around. There is no one to be found. I am at my worst.

Suddenly, as comforting as a soft warm blanket,
Your silent love captures my aching heart.
I hear within the depths of my soul,
"Fear not my child, I am with you.
I love you, and I am here to comfort you and dry your tears."

Like a little child whose daddy has reassured her, I feel whole again.
My heart has felt the depth of Your touch.
I walk to the window and look outside.
The night is still, and there is a calm that stretches over the horizon.
I am free and alive. My world is safe again.
You are my God and we are one.

Early the next morning before dawn I got up and decided to go to the hospital. Since he was in the intensive care unit, I was only allowed to visit him at certain hours. He was going in for surgery today, and I wanted to be there ahead of time. I sat in the waiting room for 2 hours before they let me go into his room. When I went in, he was asleep. I was so happy to see him. I sat down next to his bed and took his hand. "Bobby, I miss you, please answer me, let me know that you hear me." To my amazement, he opened his eyes and smiled at me. I asked him how he felt. His voice was like a whisper; he said, "Dawn, I am so happy you're here, don't worry about me, I love you." I started to weep and told him that no matter what happened,

God was with him, and so was I. I asked him if he believed that Jesus was watching over him. His eyes watered up, and he said yes. After that, they came and took him out on a stretcher to the operating room. Once again, I went into the waiting room to wait. When he came out of surgery, they brought him back into the intensive care room and hooked him up to an IV, a heart monitor and a few other machines I had never seen before. They told me that he was heavily sedated and needed to rest. They asked me to leave, and once again told me they would call me if they had any news.

    I got home and turned off my phone. If I was going to get any rest, I needed complete silence. I was feeling so overwhelmed and frightened; I didn't want to speak to anyone. I woke up the next morning with such a burden in my heart; I felt like throwing up. I called the hospital, and they connected me with the nurses' station in the intensive care unit. I asked the person on the other end, "How is my husband Bobby?" Then I heard the words, "I'm very sorry, but your husband passed away last night." All I could say was, "Thank you for letting me know." I hung up the phone. It felt like the blood had been drained out of my body. I was numb, I couldn't wrap my brain around the news I just received. How could my husband be dead at 48? If you ever lost a close loved one, you know exactly what I'm talking about. Those words are life altering. It is one of the most helpless feelings in the world to know this was something that I couldn't change or fix. It was going to take time to heal. This would be a huge test of my faith. Would I rely on God to go into the deep crevices of my heart and bring restoration to my pain, or would I allow myself to become hostile and bitter?

14

New Beginnings

The weeks following Bobby's death felt like a lifetime. I had to take care of funeral arrangements, paperwork with the insurance company, and a whole host of other responsibilities that go along with the death of a spouse. I was too busy to think of myself. After all the details were attended to, the reality of my loss came crashing down on me like a tornado. In my confusion and desperation, I cried out to God. It was hard to pray; the only thing I could get out was, "Father, You know what I'm going through; the feelings of loss and loneliness that I'm experiencing, if I ever needed Your comfort and direction, it's right now." Even though I felt like I was walking through a dark tunnel, I sensed the presence of the Lord; I knew He was going to walk with me through this grieving process. I took comfort in His Word that said, "I will never leave you or forsake you." (Hebrews 13:5). Why would I doubt Him when He's always been faithful to me in the past?

The house was really quiet. For the first time, I could hear every sound; the boards on the floor creaking as I walked, the cars passing by, the owls hooting at night. Life had come to a standstill and I knew things would never be the same. For the first couple of months, I only left the house if it was absolutely necessary. I didn't even want to be around people. I didn't want pity, I needed direction. Bobby's death reinforced in me how fragile life is; there are no absolutes; death can happen when its least expected. I spent my days sitting on the futon chair in my bedroom looking out my backdoor, listening for direction, and treasuring my time with my kitties that were able to sense my grief…what a tremendous comfort they were to me. Even though I was hurting, God's peace was indescribable. During this dark period, I wrote my best poetry. My feelings were so raw; writing once again became my solace.

Although I was still grieving, I believed it was time to move forward. I started to feel the need to be around people; I knew it was time to go back to church and start new friendships. I knew from past experiences that helping other people while I'm hurting has helped me in the past. Every Friday night, and Sundays, I would take the Staten Island Ferry to Times Square Church in Manhattan. I decided that I wanted to teach Bible studies. By teaching the Word of God, I could use my gift for encouraging others while getting direction for myself at the same time. In order to be eligible to teach, the Church required a six month commitment of taking ministry classes on Friday nights. When I had completed the courses, they gave me a certificate and informed me that I was now eligible to apply to be a teacher in the New Believers class. There was only one spot, and I was up against 300 people for the job. I filled out a lengthy, detailed application, and asked my course teacher if she would put in a good word for me. We had become friends during that six month period I had been taking the classes, and I knew that she believed in my ability to teach and counsel. Since I had been to Bible College; I believed I would have an edge in my favor when they made their determination. I received a letter in the mail informing me that an interview had been set up. I felt very uncomfortable with the prospect of being interviewed—I've never been a fan of confrontation. When I walked in the room, there were eight people waiting for me. Three of them were pastors from the church, and the others were elders. While the interview went on for over an hour, I was blasted with questions about myself and the Bible. I was so anxious during the interview; when I walked out, I thought to myself, "You'll never be hired for the position, you were too nervous." They told me they would inform me by letter in two weeks.

I decided it was time to go back to work. Sitting in the house and focusing on my pain was not doing me one drop of good; it was only hindering me from moving on—I also needed the money. I went to a temporary employment agency, and applied for a position as a legal secretary. I met with one of the interviewers who told me there was a spot in a large law firm on Fifth Avenue across from the Plaza Hotel in Manhattan. He informed me that they were really picky about the "temps," and I would have to go for an interview in the Human Resources Department of the law firm. This is not the usual procedure with temp jobs, but I was willing to do whatever it took to get work. I showed up for the interview in a black tailored suit with black pumps, and gave my resume to the woman who was interviewing me. She greeted me with a forced smile and told me to sit down. She asked me the usual round of questions, and after she was satisfied, she inquired when I would be ready to start. Judging from her cold, distant attitude, I was shocked that she was making an offer. Happily, I responded, "right away." The next day I showed up for work; the assistant in the human resources department escorted me to the desk of the secretary out on maternity leave that I was assigned to fill in for. The attorney I was assisting was one of the partners in the firm. He looked me over; his eyes darting up and down my body; he cracked a few jokes, and asked me to come in with a pad to take dictation. I had trouble keeping up with him at first; I was not accustomed to his style, but after a few days, we were getting along well together, since I had picked up my pace. I was grateful to be working again. I appreciated this new routine that took my mind off missing Bobby. The hard part for me was coming home to an empty house. I no longer had Bobby's quick inviting smile to greet me when I entered the house. He was always so happy to see me; grinning from ear to ear; giving me a "welcome home" kiss. Yet, in spite of my loss, God poured out his grace and mercy in huge measures. His presence was with me, and His favor was on me. In spite of my pain, the Lord was giving me the strength I needed emotionally to move on with my life. I was finding out that His light always shines brightest in the darkness.

  I was still waiting to hear the results of the interview at Times Square Church. I came home every day and ran to the mailbox. It was approaching three weeks since I had the interview, and still hadn't heard any news. It was a Saturday afternoon; I came home with my friend Tina after spending the day shopping together. I went to the mailbox, and there was the letter from the Church. I was so nervous, I asked Tina to open the envelope and tell me what it said. She tore open the letter. It was hard to discern from her face what was written in it; I was screaming inside, "Lord, please let it be a yes." Finally she looked at me; her face was beaming; she handed over the letter and said, "Dawn, you made it! They have decided in your favor. You got the job." I grabbed the letter out of her hand; I read the contents savoring every word as if it was a succulent, juicy steak. "Halleluiah, I screamed jumping up and down, God is so good; I can't believe they chose me." Getting this position as a teacher in the New Believers class meant more to me than getting a job. I wanted to be an encouragement to the young women coming into the church who were seeking a relationship with the Lord. God had been so gracious and faithful to me; in my gratitude I wanted to give back. I knew that it was only because of His strength that I was able to make this kind of progress after so much loss.

Subsequent to working temporary at the law firm for three months, they cut down my days since the woman I was filling in for came back from maternity leave. They told me they could still use my services, but only as a floater. I wasn't happy about that since I needed to work full-time to pay for my expenses. The days I wasn't working were not very productive. I would walk around the house feeling like I no longer belonged there; I was harping too much on losing Bobby. I had a hard time focusing because of the loneliness, and the pain was still churning in my stomach. It's not that I wasn't appreciative of what the Lord was doing for me; I made a lot of improvement in a short period of time, but I was still feeling very broken and isolated without him.

After four months of temping part-time, I was home one Monday sitting in my usual hanging out spot; my futon chair. I was praying; I asked, "Lord I need to work full-time. Would you please open a door for me?" As soon as I finished the prayer, the phone rang. I picked it up and heard a man's voice I didn't recognize, asking me if I was Dawn Dreyfuss. I said, "Yes, you're speaking to her." He replied, "A year ago you sent a resume to the Renco Group for a position as an administrative assistant. That job was taken, but we have a new position we're looking to fill. It's a brand new spot; I was looking through our resume folder when I came across your resume. I was impressed with your qualifications; are you still looking for work?"

I was so shocked, I almost dropped the phone. I replied, "I certainly am."

He inquired, "Do you have an updated resume that you can send me?"

Trying to contain my enthusiasm so as not to come off desperate, I said, "I can update it today. I have a computer at home."

Sounding very pleased, he replied, "I look forward to receiving it. After I review it, I will call you to come in for an interview."

"Yes I said, I look forward to hearing from you again… have a great day." I put down the phone, jumped up out the chair, and started running back in forth in the house, screaming with excitement, "Lord, this is a miracle." Wow! I was overwhelmed by the goodness of God. Once again, He was showing me how much He loved me. He not only heard my prayer; He answered it immediately. I was more excited about His instant response to my prayer, than the job itself. At this point, you might be thinking, "That's all good and well for you, but would God do the same thing for me?" Absolutely! As I mentioned earlier, God is no respecter of persons. What He did for me, He will do for anyone who turns to Him for guidance. It's His good pleasure to bless His children. It says in James 1:17 "Every good gift and every perfect gift is from above; it comes down from the Father of all light, in Whom there can be no variation." God knows what we need before we even ask Him. Do we trust when we pray that He will answer us? Do we think God is too busy to care about our needs? For me, I was alone and desperate. Who else did I have to depend on but the Lord? He promises in Romans 8:28 "We are assured and know that [God being a partner in our labor], all things work together and are [fitting into a plan] for good to those who love God and are called according to [His] design and purpose" What a wonderful promise to stand on. Imagine having the Creator of the universe being a partner with us in all our endeavors? When we do things according to God's will, we can't help but succeed.

The Renco Group received my updated resume, and a day later I got a call asking me to come in for an interview. I had done some research on the company, and found out it was an extremely prosperous, fast growing company that was family owned. The day of my interview, I was nervous, but very excited. I went through my closet examining every possible outfit that was appropriate. I remember spending a humungous amount of time meticulously examining every skirt, jacket and shirt till I felt satisfied. I choose a long black wool skirt, a white tailored shirt, and a pin stripped black and white jacket that fit snugly around my hips, but looked professional enough for an interview. I left the house, took the Staten Island Ferry, and when I got downtown, I caught the R train going uptown.

The office was in the NBC building—30 Rockefeller Plaza...very snazzy place! I got off the elevator and entered an office that looked like something out of Architectural Digest Magazine. The waiting room was impeccably furnished with a long cherry wood reception desk, antique tables, beautiful upholstered chairs, and a magnificent woven Persian rug covering the floor. I was impressed. Fifteen minutes later, a tall, dignified man came out and introduced himself—he was the same person I had spoke to on the phone. He escorted me to his office which was as large as my living room, tastefully furnished, overlooking a view of Manhattan to die for.

We shook hands; he gave me a big friendly smile; then

proceeded to ask me detailed questions that were not typical of other interviews I had been to previously. He told me he had looked over my resume, and wanted me to tell him more about myself. At first I wasn't sure how to respond; did he want to know about my personal life, or my business experience? I decided to play it safe and tell him about both. I elaborated on my administrative background; then I told him about Bobby's passing. He listened very intently to me speak, not interrupting me once. When I looked into his eyes, I saw a man with a great big heart; when he heard about my loss, his eyes got watery; I had touched a soft spot. I knew we had made a connection. Immediately, I felt comfortable with him; I thought to myself, "If he is any indication of how the people are in this company, I want in."

After we finished speaking, he told me to sit tight while he went to fetch the vice president of finance; he was the man I'd be working for. I waited for about 5 minutes before both men came back into the office. In walked a grey haired, distinguished gentleman who gave me a quick smile; his warm manner made me feel right at home. The three of us talked for about 15 minutes; we discussed my administrative background, my goals professionally, and the company's mission statement. The conversation between us was so light-hearted, I felt like I was conversing with friends. After the interview was over, they escorted me to an empty desk to take a typing test. When I was done, I was escorted back to the waiting room, thanked for coming in, and told they would be in touch with me in the next few days. When I left the office, I was exuberant; I felt confident that I had made a good impression on them. From what they told me about the company and the benefits, I knew this position would be a great fit for me. Now, I just had to wait it out till I heard back from them.

NEW BEGINNINGS

While waiting for an answer from the Renco Group, I continued to work temp at the law firm as a floater. One week later, while at work, I got a call from the Renco Group offering me the position. Of course, I said yes, inquiring when I should start. Since it was a few days before the Christmas holidays, they told me January 2nd. I hung up the phone feeling elated. Reflecting back, I couldn't believe that in just 7 months time God had done so much to put my life back together. Now, I had a great church to go to with new friends, the opportunity to teach bible studies; and a job with excellent pay at a prestigious company. What more could I ask for? I had done the legwork by putting myself out there, but it was the Lord who had opened the doors and gave me these awesome opportunities. I decided that it was time to celebrate; I was going to rejoice and have a good time during the holidays. I made plans with friends to go into to Manhattan to see the Christmas tree at Rockefeller Plaza; then we'd eat downstairs at the Rock Center Cafe while watching the skaters and wrapping up the day walking down Fifth Avenue while looking at all the gorgeous wintery scenes in the windows of Saks Fifth Avenue and Macy's. This was a New Year that I had a lot to celebrate.

On January 2nd, after enjoying the Christmas holidays, I showed up for work excited and ready to get started. While being escorted to my desk, I took a quick look at the surroundings in this incredibly posh office. I noticed the entire office had state of the art amenities. All the cabinets were brand new; cherry wood with brass handles. There was plush carpeting on the floor; the conference room was immense—the table was so huge, it looked like King Arthur's roundtable. As I walked around, taking it all in, I thought I had died and gone to heaven. I had never seen an office this elegant. Dennis, the man who interviewed me, took me around and introduced me to the entire staff. The people reflected the office; sophisticated, and dressed like they just stepped out of Vogue. I was briefed about the rules and regulations of the office, and given my first assignment.

The woman sitting across from me named Janice was a striking blonde, witty and helpful, a "chatty Kathy" type. From the start, she reached out to me, and we became good friends. We would go out to lunch together; we fancied shopping, trying on clothes, and getting some much needed exercise after sitting all morning. One particular lunch hour, we were conversing about our families. I opened up and told her that I hadn't spoken to my parents in almost a decade. I gave her a brief explanation for the break in our relationship. As soon as I was finished sharing, she told me, "Dawn you have to call your parents." That was the last thing I wanted to hear. I thought that she would be sympathetic; I certainly didn't want to hear her telling me to call them after all the rejection I had experienced from them when I married Bobby. I voiced my objections to her; but she held her ground, and reiterated again, "They are your parents; you need to call them. If they have already rejected you, what do you have to lose if they don't want to speak to you?" I told her I would think about it.

Even though I didn't want to admit it, I knew she was right. After all God had taught me about forgiveness, I knew that in order to move forward spiritually and emotionally, I needed to confront my issues with my mother. Yet, the pain was so deep. I thought to myself; "Every time I attempted reconciliation with her in the past, it always led to more disappointment. Do I really want to open that wound again, especially now that things were going so well for me?" Yet I didn't want to be a hypocrite; how was I going to teach the women in the new believers' class about surrendering to God, when I was still harboring resentment toward my mother? I decided that I would take the chance of being disappointed and call, but first, I needed God to soften my heart toward her. For me, this was a spiritual battle. I prayed for the strength and courage to make the call. During the next couple of weeks I consistently cried out to the Lord, asking, "Please Father, change my heart and my feelings towards my mother; give me the ability to lay down the hurt and forgive her once again. You have forgiven me for the times in my life when I harbored bitterness; teach me how to love her with the same love you have shown me." In those weeks, these questions kept coming to my mind: "Do you have any love left for your mother? Is she deserving of your love? Will she hurt you once again?" If you have struggled with these emotions, you know how difficult it can be to let it go. After reflecting on these painful questions, and seeking God's wisdom, I decided, "Yes," I still care about her and my father. I've learned that love comes with a cost; there is always the possibility of pain and rejection. But what is the alternative? Should I shut everyone out every time I feel rejected? If I did that, I would have no one in my life. I learned that at times people hurt and reject us; that is the fabric of relationships. In fact, it's usually the people we love the most; they're the ones who can cause us the greatest hurt. After much speculation, I decided to take Janice's advice and give them a call.

I didn't know if the last phone number I had for my parents would still be in service. After all, it was over ten years since we had last spoken. I figured, "Oh what the heck, let me try it." The phone rang, and I heard my father's voice on the other end. I was so nervous, my hands were shaking.

"Hi dad, this is Dawn. How are you doing?" For a couple of seconds, there was silence on the other end. I started to wonder if this was a good idea.

I heard my father say, "Dawn is that really you?"

"Yes," I chimed in. "How are you and mother doing?"

He said, "Fine, let me put your mother on the phone."

She picked up the phone, and in true Rita style, blurted out, "Dawn, we have been so worried about you, why haven't you called us in all these years?"

I didn't want to get into a dispute, so I bypassed the question and told her that Bobby had died.

She didn't sound shocked; she asked me; "What was the reason for his passing?"

"Liver failure," I answered.

"Are you working?" she inquired. I tried to be patient in spite of her bombarding me with questions. "We sold the condo in Boca Raton and bought a house in West Palm Beach."

"Great, I'm glad you're doing well. How is Robert?" Unfortunately, over the years, my brother and I had lost touch. I realized while I was talking to my parents that I really missed my family.

"He's doing terrific; they just bought a new house." My brother had met his wife in college, and they had adopted two children, a boy and a girl. "When can you come down to visit?" my mother asked.

"I don't know, I'm working full time, I'm not eligible to take a vacation till I'm with the company for six months."

"We'll send you a ticket," she offered.

"Okay, I said, "Let me put some things in order, and I'll let you know when I can come and see you."

"Dawn, I'm so glad to hear your voice; you sound like you're doing very well;" my dad said in a soft whisper. That really touched my heart; I knew my father was sincere by the tone of his voice.

"Thanks, dad, I missed you guys. It was so hard for me to be all alone after Bobby died."

NEW BEGINNINGS

"Dawn, we're very delighted you called. We hope you can come down during the Christmas holidays to visit. We'll call Robert and let him know that we heard from you."

"Thanks dad, it was wonderful to talk with you and mom. I'll call again soon." When we hung up, I started to weep. My relationship with my parents had always been so volatile. Maybe, now that I'm older and hopefully wiser, we can bridge the gap, and start creating some new memories. I realized that no matter what happens in a family, there is a love and loyalty that never totally evaporates no matter how much hurt there is. "Lord, I said, I'm so grateful that you gave me the courage to contact my parents. Talking to them was not as painful as I thought it would be; good or bad, they are my parents, and I want them in my life. There are not enough words in my limited human vocabulary to convey to You how grateful I am for all you have done for me."

My parents called me a week later and told me they had spoken to my brother and told him that I called. They said that he was planning on coming down to Florida for the Christmas holidays with the kids, and he hoped that I would be able to come too. I was really excited to hear that. The last time I had seen his son Jared he was an infant; his daughter Jaimie, I had never met.

"Yes, I'm anxious to see everyone, I'll call the airlines and make arrangements," I said joyfully.

My dad replied; "Get your ticket and we'll send you the money."

"Okay dad, I'll call you as soon as I make the arrangements." As soon as I got off the phone with them, I called American Airlines and booked my flight for the Christmas holidays. I made a mental note to thank my friend Janice at work. If it hadn't been for her prompting, I wouldn't have called them.

OUT OF THE DARKNESS INTO THE LIGHT

I informed my company that I was going to take vacation during the Christmas holidays, and they agreed to my request. Two weeks before my trip was due, I was so excited; I was running around like "a chicken without a head." I wanted to buy presents for everyone. I got Jaimie dolls and teddy bears, for Jared, I bought a couple of "boy" games, I got my dad p.j.'s, since my brother is a "fashionista," I got him a watch and Tommy Hilfinger cologne. My mother had asked me to get her brownies from a bakery she loved on Madison Avenue; that was understandable since her first love is chocolate.

Finally, the day arrived for me to go to see my family. I needed an entire suitcase just to carry the presents. I had so much stuff; you would think I was going on a worldwide tour. Getting dressed was a nightmare; since I hadn't seen them in so long, I wanted to look my best. I tried on every pair of jeans and tee shirts I owned. Finally with all my suitcases in tow, I headed for the airport. The plane ride was relaxing; I indulged in my usual plane activities: drinking cokes and watching movies. After 2 ½ hours we landed in Palm Beach airport. When I got off the plane, I was feeling excited and apprehensive all at the same time. There were so many questions running through my mind; "How would I feel spending time with them after all these years? Would I get along with my mother? Could we really bury the past and start over?" Upon arrival, I picked up my bags and left the airport; when I walked outside, there was my father and brother standing outside the car waving at me. My first reaction when I greeted them was pure delight. I could tell from their smiles and hugs they were genuinely happy to see me. When we got in the car, they told me that my mother and the kids were at home waiting for me. The conversation on the way to my parent's house was casual and nonchalant. We engaged in small talk about the weather and my flight. After an hour drive, due to the traffic, we arrived at my parent's house. My father got my bags and told me to go inside. My mother greeted me at the door. The second I saw her, my heart skipped a beat. It was at that moment I realized I had forgiven her; she was grinning from ear to ear and I was doing the same. I could feel her warmth, and knew already that this trip would be a memorable one. I spent the next week hanging out with the kids, enjoying my mother's cooking, going to the beach with my brother, and taking pleasure in the company of my family for the first time in many years. Everyone was at their best, and made a terrific effort to get along. I tried to talk to my mother about what had happened between us in the past, but she was not ready to open up to me. I came to the conclusion that I might never get the answers or the resolution I wanted from her. For her to be open and honest with me, she had to first be willing to be honest with herself. That would require her to take responsibility for her part in our broken relationship. I had done the work in my heart by admitting to myself that I had not been a great a daughter; now in order for us to bridge the gap, she had to do her own work. Yet, in spite of the walls that still remained between us, I was delighted that I had been given the chance to spend the time with them.

I spent the last night before going back to New York reflecting on how far I had come since my days of being a broken, angry, mess of a person. From the day I had committed my life to the Lord to the present time, God has transformed me into a human being I could finally respect and be proud of. The road had been paved by many mishaps; I'd made numerous mistakes along the way, but in spite of all that, God had been faithful to His promises. Like a loving father, His patience and steadfast love would always shine through; upholding me, encouraging me, and guiding me along the rocky roads of this unpredictable journey called life.

15

Restoration—
God's Faithfulness

Although I continued to miss Bobby, time does heal the heart; life goes on, and things did get better. Two years after Bobby's passing, I decided it was time to find a new place to live. I was looking through the ads in the newspaper (the internet didn't exist yet), when I came across an advertisement, saying, "I'm looking to sell my kitchen table, and to rent my 1 bedroom apartment." It seemed odd to me that someone would be advertising to sell a table and rent an apartment in the same advertisement. Usually, the two are listed separately. It intrigued me, and I decided to call and check it out. When I called, a woman picked up the phone. I told her my name and the reason for the call. She asked me where I lived, and what kind of an apartment I was looking to rent.

"A large 1 bedroom in good condition," I answered.

She said, "Great, why don't you come over, and we'll talk about it."

"That sounds like a plan," I responded. We made plans for

the following Sunday to get together. I hung up and wondered to myself, "Could this be the answer to my prayers?"

That Sunday, my friend and I piled into his car (I wanted a second opinion), and took off for Princess Bay, the opposite end of Staten Island. When I arrived in the neighborhood, I was pleased to notice that the houses appeared to be well taken care of, and that the lawns were meticulously manicured. She answered the door with a smile on her face and told me to come in. She was young, in her 20's, and proceeded to tell me that she was living with her fiancé, his brother and wife. Since the apartment was too small for four people, they needed to find a new place. She showed me around from room to room. It was a large one bedroom apartment, exactly what I was looking for. The apartment was well laid out, and it was in great shape. She told me they wanted to move in the next month or two, and if I was interested, she would speak to the landlord about me; he lived in New Rochelle. "Lives in New Rochelle, I grew up in New Rochelle," I excitedly announced to her. Maybe this was God's way of saying; "Dawn this is your new place." "That would be fantastic, I told her, I really like the apartment, and would be interested in moving in as soon as possible."

"I'll call the landlord tonight, but I still have to find another apartment before I move from this one," she said.

After she spoke to the landlord she called me back and asked me if I was willing to meet with him. "Of course," I said. Two weeks later, Mr. Pappalorois and I met for lunch in the restaurant in my office building. Since Diane had given him a description of what I looked like, he immediately recognized me. He gave me a warm, generous smile and sat down. He proceeded to take out a piece of paper to write; then he went into his suitcase and pulled out a standard lease.

"So, you work in this building?" he inquired. Before I could answer he bombarded me with another round of questions. "How long have you been working here? Why are you interested in moving? Will you be renting the apartment alone? When do you want to move in?" he interrogated without taking a breather. Chuckling, I looked intently at him and answered each one of his questions. When I was done, he apologized for being so direct, eased up, and asked me if I wanted to go over the lease with him.

"Of course," I said, "That's why I'm here." He proceeded to read all the details and fine print in the lease and asked me if I had any questions. "No," I replied.

"Okay, then sign at the bottom, I'll make you a copy; when Diane finds an apartment, you can move in. I require one month's security, and one month's rent upfront."

"Fine, can I give that to you by check before I move in?"

"We have a deal," he remarked joyfully.

Two months later I moved into my new home. What a crazy, hectic day that turned out to be! I had ordered bedroom furniture from an antique shop that was being delivered that same day; a television set and wall unit from Sears; plus the furniture I was taking from my other apartment; two cars full of boxes; and my three cats in cages, Max, Sadie, and Cody. Thank God I had my three closest friends to help calm me down from all the tension. Also, Diane had offered me the use of her friend's truck to help bring some additional items. Finally, after ten hours of madness, the job was done; I was all moved in and ready to embark upon my new life in my new home.

I had a ball going shopping and paying attention to every detail while decorating my cozy little nest. Even my children with fur were adjusting to their new territory. I had to give all the glory to God; He had taken the ashes of my life; my loss, my pain; and made something beautiful from it. If it hadn't been for his favor, I would never have found the apartment. Now, I had great hope for what the future was to bring. Everything was looking up!

After much talk in the media, the Internet finally arrived on the scene. I purchased a new computer, logged on, and decided it was time to explore ways to make my poetry known to the public. I started by searching for Christian publications. It was quite a challenge since the Internet was in its infant stages, and there wasn't much of a market yet for my work online.

One particular morning, I got up, brewed my coffee; (can't start the day without my caffeine fix); and starting to search for new sites for my poems. I had logged on to the Reader's Digest site when an advertisement popped up for Christian personals. "Christian personals," I laughed out loud. "Is there really such thing as Christian personals?" Back then, online dating was considered a "no, no." I was just about to X out of the site, when I sensed the strongest urge to probe further. I felt as if something was guiding my hand instead of my mind to investigate. Puzzled by the implications of finding a man on the computer, my curiosity forced me to succumb to the temptation to explore my prospects. I figured, "Okay, it can't hurt to look; what do I have to lose?" The page was very user friendly in the way it was organized; all I had to do was look for men in my area who were in my age group. I typed in New York City. Wow! I was flabbergasted; it was loaded with pictures and profiles of guys from all over New York City. After browsing through quite a few profiles, I found one that caught my interest. He was 55 years old, (I was 49 at the time), he lived in Queens, he was a writer, and a cook by profession. "Yay!" I remarked to myself, "That sounds like someone of interest that I could relate to; a creative person." After much trepidation, I responded by sending him an E-mail. I thought with amusement, "Who knows if I'll hear from him, but it will be interesting to see where this leads." It had been 5 years since Bobby had passed away, and I had been praying that God would bring a godly man into my life.

The following day I logged on without a thought as to whether or not I would get a response from this stranger online. While going through my E-mail, I noticed a name I was not familiar with. I was somewhat apprehensive to open it up since I had heard about the horrors of getting a virus from unknown mail that might have malware attached. Then, it occurred to me that it could be from that guy on Christian personals that I responded to. Sure enough, to my surprise he had answered me rather quickly. Scanning through the E-mail, my eyes locked onto something he had wrote that startled me. He mentioned that he was a widower and his wife had died in 1996 at 48 years old. Astonished by those words, I almost fell off my seat. This was so bizarre, Bobby had died in 1996 and he was 48 years old when he passed away. Not knowing what to make of this information; I took it as a sign from God that He might be trying to tell me something. After all, in the last five years I had grown and matured spiritually and was receptive to sharing my life again with the right person.

We E-mailed back and forth for a couple of months; sharing our spiritual life, our values; interests, and the back stories of our lives. I was growing fond of John; appreciating his love for his grown daughters and eagerly awaiting every new article he would send me about different topics in the Bible he was passionate about. When he gave me his phone number and told me to give him a call, I took him up on the offer. I waited expectantly while the phone rang on his end, wondering what this man that I had been communicating with digitally would have to say. When he picked up, I was pleased to hear his charming, engaging Greek accent saying hello.

"Hi John, this is Dawn, how's it going?" I responded automatically.

"Dawn, I'm so glad you called." During our lengthy conversation, I was fascinated listening to him converse with ease about himself; answering all my questions with wit and tact. When we had finished exchanging our heart-to-heart dialogue, we made a date to meet that Sunday, which was Memorial Day, in front of the Museum of Modern Art in Manhattan. After hanging up the phone, I thought to myself how pleasant it will be to find out more about this man with the interesting Greek accent who was so entertaining to converse with.

That Sunday, when I arrived in front of the Museum of Modern Art; there was John a handsome, bearded man dressed like someone from the 1960's waiting for me. My first thought was, "He's cute, but those clothes have to go; he would make good friend material." I inquired after profiling him, "Are you John?"

"Yes, Dawn," he responded smiling like the Cheshire Cat. We decided to bypass the museum and go to Starbuck's for coffee and further conversation. Effortlessly, we talked and talked for hours. As I listened to him speak with his charming smile and cute Greek accent, I perceived him to be a straightforward man with a strong character. Although I liked what I saw and heard; he make me feel somewhat uncomfortable with his leering eyes and alluring smile that looked like it was painted on his face permanently; but I hadn't dated in so long; what did I know about courting in this modern age? Yet, as I examined his piercing brown eyes and watched his full lips construct his words, I was captivated by his boyish good looks. What I really found fascinating was his Greek background; this was my first time getting to know a Greek man. After spending the good part of the day together, I drove back to Staten Island very pleased with our encounter.

OUT OF THE DARKNESS INTO THE LIGHT

After getting together numerous times in Queens, I decided to invite him to visit me in Staten Island. The day he was due to show up, I spent the morning cleaning the house and pampering myself to get everything ready for his arrival. In mid afternoon, a couple of hours before John was supposed to arrive, out of nowhere I experienced a sharp, crippling pain in my right foot. The pain was so excruciating I fell to the ground. When I tried to get up, I couldn't put any weight on that foot. I had experienced something similar seven years before when I was diagnosed with sciatica; a condition springing from damaged disks in my back. I couldn't believe this was happening to me; I didn't know what to do since I was all alone in the house. Finally, after many painful tries, I was able to lift myself up off the floor. I knew that if this was in fact sciatica, I needed to get immediate treatment. I called a cab and told the driver to take me to Staten Island University Hospital which was close to my house. Thankfully, the emergency room was empty when I arrived, and I was seen immediately by the doctor on call. After many questions and an X-ray, the doctor confirmed my worst fears; I had sciatica. Leaving the hospital with medication, I called another cab and headed for the pharmacy in my neighborhood. I got my prescription filled for painkillers; I hated to take them because of my prior issues with addiction; but I was feeling so much anguish, I didn't have any choice. Annoyingly, I kept thinking, "This is a disaster and the timing can't be any worse, John is due to arrive any minute and I can't even walk." I couldn't put any weight on my right foot, when I did, I experienced such throbbing, it brought tears to my eyes. I looked like an oversized bunny hopping around on one foot. Moments later the doorbell rang; I opened the door with a pathetic expression on my face while attempting to appear pleased that he had come. Instantly, he knew something was wrong and inquired in a concerned voice, "What happened to you?"

As I chronicled the details of my affliction, he helped me sit down and asked me what he could do to help me. Flabbergasted by my helpless state, I smiled and told him, "You can get me a glass of water out of the fridge, and help me to the couch to lie down."

Even though I was bed bound since I couldn't walk, I still was able to laugh and converse with John effortlessly. We talked about our faith; sharing how God had come into our lives and brought transformation. John shared with me how as a young boy growing up on a farm in the small village of Ramata, Greece, he was always interested in having a relationship with God. He grew up in the Greek Orthodox Church; not feeling satisfied by his "dry, dead religion" that was works orientated, he wanted something more. The priests would sing the psalms, go about their rituals and instruct him regarding all the things he had to do to satisfy a God who seemed so distant. He was a seeker like me; always searching for the God he did not know. He came to America in 1968 looking to fulfill the American Dream. Watching television, he would listen to the preachers who promised him that God was just a prayer away. Finally, after much speculation about his life and sinful nature, he decided to get on his knees and ask the Lord to come in and make something significant out of his life. Little by little God started to revolutionize his world view; he reported how his desires, his plans and everything concerning his existence began to alter. Hearing him speak so passionately about His transformed life in Jesus Christ was like a breath of fresh air to me. It made me want to grow closer to this man who was setting off a spark in my heart that had been dead since Bobby died.

For the next three months I felt like an invalid from the sciatica which caused me to be bedridden. To my great dismay, due to my prolonged physical condition, I was forced to leave the job that I loved. I was only able to hop to the bathroom on one leg; it took all my strength to get up and feed the cats; and answer the door when food was being delivered. John became like an angel to me; he would come every Friday after work, driving 2 hours in rush hour traffic to lend me a hand. He would go food shopping for me, clean the house, cook the food and take care of my pets. I was enthralled by this man who was willing, in spite of my condition, to do whatever it took to make me feel comfortable while waiting to get better. What woman wouldn't be? During this time of being bedridden, my prayers and time with God became all the more precious to me. I had a choice; I could have been resentful and blamed God for my helpless condition, but instead, I choose to ask, "Lord, what do You want to teach me; what do I need to learn from this lesson?" Yes, I hated to be in pain and feel so completely helpless, but I sure didn't want to waste whatever message I needed to be taught by whining and complaining. I knew God was a healer and He would raise me up and strengthen my faith through this affliction. My favorite words in the Bible to meditate on during that time of affliction were 2 Corinthians 9-10 "But He said to me, My grace—My favor and loving-kindness and mercy are enough for you, [that is, sufficient against any danger and to enable you to bear the trouble manfully]; for My strength and power are made perfect—fulfilled and completed and show themselves more effective—in [your] weakness. Therefore, I will all the more gladly glory in my weaknesses and infirmities, that the strength and power of Christ, the Messiah, may rest—yes, may pitch a tent [over] and dwell upon me! So, for the sake of Christ, I am well

RESTORATION—GOD'S FAITHFULNESS

pleased and take pleasure in infirmities, insults, hardships, persecutions, perplexities and distresses; for when I am weak (in human strength), then am I [truly strong—able, powerful in divine strength." These are some of the scriptures that helped me get through that extremely difficult time.

Finally, after three months, I woke up one morning and the sciatica was gone; as quickly as it came, that's how quickly it departed. I never realized how much my health and well being meant to me until it was taken away. I was ecstatic to be able to get out of bed and walk around my house. I was feeling fully alive and in the moment; the mundane everyday chores became a time of singing and dancing; I was celebrating life. What freedom I felt getting in my car and driving; going to the supermarket; doing the laundry. All the mundane things that I had taken for granted, now meant the world to me. During my time in bed, once again, the Lord showed me the importance of gratitude, and depending upon Him for everything. In spite of all my growth, I can still be extremely stubborn and fiercely independent. Every now and then, God has to get my attention to bring me back to the center of His will. I have the tendency to make quick decisions and go full throttle forward without weighing the consequences. Anyone who has a strong choleric temperament knows exactly what I'm talking about. I'm learning to take a breath, pray and look at all my options before making decisions that I'll be sorry for later on. To me, maturity is not a about chronological age; it's about taking the experiences in my life and learning from them; gaining the wisdom to do better when I know better.

John was thrilled to learn that I was back on my feet. Instead of coming over to wait on me hand and foot, now we were able to do things we never got a chance to enjoy while I was bedridden. It was the little things that he did that meant so much to me: bringing me flowers, taking me out to eat, going to church together, playing miniature golf, taking a walk, whatever we did had so much meaning to me. We were sharing our hearts together, talking about what was important in our lives: what we wanted to accomplish, struggles we had in the past, and plans for the future. I was starting to wonder if this was the man God wanted me to be with. He had certainly proved that he was dependable, yet inside I still had my doubts. Even though God had done tremendous healing in me, there were still places in my heart that had closed doors. Relationships were a scary ordeal for me. I knew in order for it to work there has to be vulnerability, transparency and risk involved. After spending the last five years alone since Bobby died, and being fairly successful, did I really want to start all over with someone else? At 49, I was very set in my ways; still self-centered and headstrong. Bobby was so giving and easy going; I didn't have to sacrifice that much with him. John had a different temperament. Even though I knew that I could count on him, I also knew that I couldn't push him around. He had a strong personality like me. I asked myself, "Could two very strong willed personalities co-exist in the same house? If we did get together, would we be banging heads all the time? Would I be taking on more than I could handle?" These were the questions I had to ask myself. In my younger years I never considered these things. If the guy was attractive and had a fun personality, I was all in. I no longer allowed myself that luxury at 49.

 John never formally asked me to marry him. After we had been going out for eight months, he started to hint at the possibility of making it official. Cristina, his daughter, was engaged at the time and had plans to marry her fiancé Nick in May. She had been living with John since his wife died. Now that she was getting married, she was planning on moving to Westchester where Nick lived. That meant that John would have the apartment to himself. His way of proposing was, "Dawn since Cristina will be getting married, you can move in." That was his way of saying let's tie the knot. I know it doesn't sound conventional or romantic, but I knew John loved me and wanted us to be together.

My response was, "This summer I'm going to Israel. If you want you can join me."

He responded, "After the school year's over we can get married; I'll pay for us to go to Israel if you're willing to go to Greece to visit my family."

"You've got a deal," I responded with elation.

When June arrived, we started to make plans to get married and go on our honeymoon. I was excited and panicky all at the same time. I tried to convince John to move into my apartment, but he didn't want to give up his job at the Board of Education. I really loved my place and hated to give it up; yet I knew that marriage to John would require me to make many sacrifices which would not be easy on my flesh. For the past five years, my wants and wishes were based solely upon what I needed; what I thought was good for me. Now, I had to make choices based upon "we." I needed a person who would stand his ground and not be passive. I like what Proverbs 14:1 says, "A wise woman builds her house, but a foolish woman tears it down with her own hands." My desire was to be that wise woman who builds her house with understanding, good judgment, kindheartedness, and compassion. My past actions had taught me that when I manipulate to get my way, it may appear like I'm winning, but if the if the other person feels taken advantage of, it will only cause resentment and strife; the end result of that game will be misery and isolation. I knew John would be a challenge for me; I was still asking myself, will I be able to rise up and do it God's way which requires compromise and negotiation, or will I rebel and go back to my old childish ways of behaving? I wanted to believe that I had matured enough spiritually to handle the challenge.

June 29, 2001, was a hot, muggy day with the air so thick it sat on me like a wet blanket. I woke up that morning with the realization that my life was about to change drastically; this was my wedding day. After much debate, John and I finally decided that it make more sense for me to move into his apartment in Queens; that way he didn't have to give up his job at the Board of Education. As I already mentioned, it was not my first choice, but I was willing to make the concession. My one bargaining tool was my cat Max. With much convincing, John's landlord finally acquiesced to my demand for Max to come and live with us. He was eight years old at the time and to me he was just as important as if he was my child. Since I didn't have any children, my pets had filled that place in my heart. Unfortunately, my Sadie had died at 10 and my Cody was living with an upstairs neighbor whose two children loved him and begged me to allow them to adopt him. Since it was our second marriage, and we were going on a long, very expensive honeymoon, we both decided that we would get married by the Justice of Peace in City Hall in Staten Island. My two closest girlfriends happily agreed to come and be witnesses. While getting dressed in my two-piece white embroidered outfit, my mind wandered back to the others that I had loved before. Each one of them had something special that would stay with me forever. The memories, good and bad, never go away. I had often heard the question pondered by friends, talk show hosts; can a person love more than one individual in a lifetime? For me, the answer was yes; each person I had shared my life with had that singular, unique quality that aroused my heart. Now, I was given the chance to love once more; to be like a caterpillar that evolves into a butterfly. I was given new wings to fly again.

My lips quivered as I whispered my wedding vows. It was quite apparent that John was just as nervous; with a smile on his face, in a soft voice, he said his "I do's." His hand was shaking as he gently slipped my gold and platinum wedding band on my third finger. After what seemed like a millennium, the Justice of the Peace pronounced us husband and wife. It was a tender moment forever etched in my heart. I might have a hard exterior at times, but when it comes to matters of the heart I'm a hopeless romantic. John leaned forward took my face in his hands and gave me a tender kiss as he gently brushed my lips. I responded with the same enthusiasm, lifted my head up and shouted, "We did it; we're married." My friends ran over to give us their sincere congratulations. When we walked out of the Court House, the four of us piled into John's car and headed to the restaurant to celebrate our new union. In spite of all my qualms, it turned out to be a fantastic, memorable day.

Two weeks later, we were ready to leave for Greece and Israel. I was ecstatic with anticipation at the prospect of going to the Holy Land. This had been on my bucket list for a long time, and now my dream to visit the land where Jesus walked was about to come true. I think I would be accurate in saying that for a Jewish person the land of Israel holds a special place in their heart. I was also excited to go to Greece to meet John's relatives. He had shared with me many stories of his childhood growing up in the little village of Ramata. The only apprehension I had was that Greece is predominately a Greek speaking country; I wondered, "How will I communicate with his family?" I didn't know one word of Greek.

After a tedious 9 hour flight, we arrived at Athens International Airport. John and I could feel the excitement rise up as we walked out of the airport and saw his sister Katrina and her husband Pete waiting for us. They greeted us with big smiles and hugs, and Katrina handed me a beautiful red rose. Even though I couldn't speak directly to them due to the language barrier; their warm hearts and appreciative greetings were unmistakable; already they made me feel like I was part of their family. I was looking forward to spending time with them in their home for the four days we would be in Athens. Once we got our suitcases in the house and unpacked, Katrina whipped up a delicious mouth watering Greek meal; we had roasted lamb with mint; latholemono (broccoli with oil and lemon); arakas me patates (dilled peas with potatoes); a salad with feta cheese and kalamata olives; and for dessert she served baklava which is a traditional Greek delight with filo dough layered with butter, cinnamon, honey and nuts. I ate till I felt like I was going to explode; I couldn't get enough of the mouth watering food she served. The conversation between John and his sister as they caught up was filled with laughter. Even though it was all Greek to me, I could sense the love and deep connection between the two of them. During my time in Athens, I had a chance to meet John's 92 year old father, his brother Nick and his wife; and Katrina's daughter Sophie, her husband and two children. There was a real sense of family and unity among them. Everyone treated me like royalty; my only frustration was not being able to participate in their conversations, although John played the role of translator quite well.

 When the four days were up, Katrina and Pete drove us to the ferry to sail to the island of Andros where John was born and raised. The ferry ride was quite extraordinary; my senses were in overdrive as I took in the grandeur and splendor of the Greek Islands. These islands are nuzzled in a circular direction around the Mediterranean Sea as far as the eye can see. After two hours, we arrived in Andros. Getting off the ferry, the first thing that caught my eye was the purity of the landscape. The houses are predominately blue and white in color, and except for the roads which are narrow, the houses sit perched in the clefts of the rocks. The streets are lined with quaint little cafes surrounding the white sandy beaches along the turquoise colored Mediterranean Sea. I had never seen anything like it, when you look into the transparent water, you can see to the bottom as the tiny little minnows make circles around your feet. I felt like I was in paradise.

We checked into one of the motels in the town of Batsi. Even though John hadn't lived in the country for 40 years, there were still some old timers who knew his family. What a fabulous time I was having; you couldn't possibly find a more romantic place to be on a honeymoon. We spent the last 3 days we had left in Andros eating delicious food, strolling along the beaches, holding hands and walking at night along the Mediterranean. I kept thinking how fortunate I was to have found someone that I could share my life with after all the pain and suffering I had experienced. It was impossible not to reflect on the goodness of God and how He had turned my life around. If it hadn't been for His faithfulness, what would have become of me? Instead, I was on my honeymoon in a gorgeous land with someone I loved.

When we left the islands, we went back to Athens to get our suitcases and get ready for our trip to Israel. During the trip to the airport, everyone was smiles as we reflected on the great time we had together. I was brought to tears as Pete kissed me and said s'agapo poly which means I love you much. Overall, it had been a memorable seven days filled with laughter, love and great food.

The flight to Israel was a short one. As soon as we arrived in

Ben Gurion Airport, my heart went pitter patter with anticipation. I was overcome with exhilaration as I thought about all the historic places I was going to see in the land of the Bible. It's amazing to me that Israel is only the size of New Jersey, yet she has the most coveted real estate in the world. Once we went through customs, we got our suitcases and tried to find the sign that said Pilgrim Tours. Within minutes, we recognized a short, thin, middle aged man looking around holding the sign for Pilgrim Tours with our names printed in bold capital letters. We went up to meet him and introduced ourselves; he told us his name was Jeff and he was going to be our tour guide. He cracked some pretty lame jokes about New Yorkers, and led us to his tour bus. As we started riding through Haifa to the hotel, I felt like I had come home; my heart was tied to this land of unique contradictions. I looked out the window and thought, "I am in the land where my ancestors made aliya (Jews who return to Israel to live); they migrated from Russia, Ukraine, throughout Europe and my own country United States to come back to their homeland." In the year 1948, on my birthday, May 14th, Israel was declared a nation; against all odds, the Jewish state was born. I could already feel the joy bubbling up inside of me at the prospect of spending the next 8 days traveling from Haifa to Tel Aviv, and then finally to Jerusalem; the city where the three major religions of the world have their center of worship, Judaism, Christianity and Islam.

As I walked along the crowded bustling streets in Haifa watching the Jewish woman scurry in and out of the shops and supermarkets, I was astounded by their sense of unity and community. Even though Hebrew is the main language of the country, I could hear young and old alike speaking both in Hebrew and English. In the monotony of their daily routine, they went about their business, exuding genuine warmth towards one another that was unmistakable. When I was making plans to come to Israel, I was cautioned by many of my friends to reconsider going due to the violence and terror in the land. Yet, as I walked along the streets, I sensed none of that. Instead I felt a great peace as I watched and listened to the locals engaging in conversations together; they were smiling and laughing as if they didn't have a care in the world. The threat of danger is there, yet the people go about their affairs with a sense of confidence that God will watch over them. Many times the media portrays the Israelites as cold, insensitive, hostile people. Instead, everywhere I went both Jews and Arabs alike made me feel right at home; they went out of their way to give directions and answer whatever questions I had. As a result of our interaction together, it changed my impression of the relationship between the Jews and Arabs. For whatever reason, the news at home portrays a different picture about the relationship between the Arabs and the Jews. In the United States many of us are told that the Jews and the Arabs in Israel hate each other; but when I sat down and talked to the men and woman of both persuasions, they told me that the stereotypes given in the media was over exaggerated. Many of them live next door to each other and their kids go to school together. In the hotels, the Arabs work right alongside the Jews; and not once did I see any dispute amongst them.

On our first day on the tour bus, along with another family of five, we all headed out to explore the city of Haifa. Haifa is the largest city in northern Israel built on the slopes of Mount Carmel. Our tour guide Jeff led the way as we trekked up Mount Carmel. I had chills in my spine as I looked around Elijah's Cave. I couldn't help but feel like I was being transported back into biblical times when I looked at the sites where the characters in the Bible interacted with God. Looking down into the valley of Megiddo, I reflected on all the bloody wars that were fought in that valley. It was on Mt. Carmel that Elijah commanded King Ahab to summon the Israelites and the prophets of Baal to come and watch while he repaired the altar of the Lord that had been torn down. He challenged the prophets of Baal to a contest to determine the true God of Israel. In spite of the 450 prophets of Baal crying out to their gods to the point of harming themselves, they got no response. When, Elijah petitioned the God of Abraham, Isaac and Jacob to show His power to the people, the Lord responded miraculously by burning up the sacrifice Elijah had offered on the altar. That settled it! All the people fell down to the ground and proclaimed that the God of Israel was indeed the true God.

After three days in Haifa, we headed toward our next destination, Tel Aviv. Tel Aviv is a city in western Israel on the Mediterranean; it is the largest city in Israel and the chief financial center. It's a stunning city with cutting-edge boutiques, restaurants, and night spots populating every block. Much like New York City, it is known as the city that never sleeps. After a full day of shopping and exploring the markets, we dined out late at night in a restaurant overlooking the Mediterranean. With the moon beaming down on the crystal clear water, we watched as the young Israelis' danced to the disco tunes of the 80's: Donna Summers, Michael Jackson, Madonna and many others that Americans cherish; they danced with an abandonment and freedom that showed that in spite of the precarious state of their country; they were free and happy to be alive. After sharing an excellent meal, we held hands and walked block after block marveling at the beautiful styles of architecture lining the streets clad with townhouses and uniquely designed office buildings. This city fed my spirit and soul. Everywhere I went, I took pleasure in seeing this beautiful land that had been built up to be a thriving city with site after site of biblical significance in just a short period of 60 years. Tel Aviv is an intoxicating mélange of sights, smells, tastes and sounds. I kept remarking to John that "I never want to leave this country that awakens my senses and makes my heart sing." I could feel the presence of God in this land of contrasts like no other place on earth. Looking into the faces of the many nationalities that come to visit this land, I saw a common thread amongst us; it didn't matter what religious beliefs we held; we all felt the magic and spark that this land exudes.

One of the sites that particularly touched my heart was a boat ride we took on the Sea of Galilee. It was a gorgeous summer day when our small group headed out to sail on the Sea of Galilee from the pier of Tiberias in Capernaum which is located in northern Israel. We took our seats on a long, narrow plank in the wooden boat and set sail into the choppy waters. What a connection I felt with the surroundings as the water sprayed in my face, and I listened to the other sailor's call out their greetings to us; fellow travelers. Then the captain cut the motor and we sat around and marveled at the landscape around us that has been kept sacred for thousands of years. In this wooden boat, resembling the ones used in ancient times, I felt like I was being transported back into a time when people depended on the wind and waves as their livelihood. It was here that Jesus walked on water (John 6:19-21), calmed the storm (Matthew 8:23-26), and showed his disciples miraculous catches of fish by telling them to cast their nets on the other side of the boat and get ready for a huge haul. While on the boat we experienced our own miracle right before our eyes. The wind was so intense; the sail got detached and spun around in the boat. It hit John directly over the right side of his face. It should have knocked him out and caused a concussion.

Thank God I was sitting next to him; I began praying and calling out for God to intervene in what could have turned out to be a disaster. He fell into my arms and his eyes rolled back in his head. Miraculously, after only a minute or two, he opened his eyes and asked me; "What happened to me, Dawn? I feel so dizzy." Praise God! I was so relieved that nothing serious happened to him. After that, the captain took the boat back to shore and John walked off as if nothing had even happened.

We spent the last four days of the trip in Jerusalem; the new and old city. As soon as we arrived in this shining city set on a hill, I knew that my time here would be the highlight of the trip. Jerusalem is the gem in Israel's crown; the place where God has put His name. In spite of all the turmoil, I felt such a tremendous sense of peace and harmony. Everywhere you turn you see olive trees. The olive trees symbolize peace, and that's why Jerusalem is called the city of peace. Walking the streets, I sensed an atmosphere of prayer and worship as I watched the Jewish men holding their prayer books, dressed in their black coats with their yarmulkes sitting securely on their heads held in place by a bobby pin. After our group had a delicious lunch of falafel with hummus on pita bread, Jeff took us to see a model replica of the old city of Jerusalem dating back to the time when Jesus went to the temple during Passover. It was uncanny how much the old city of Jerusalem thousands of years ago still resembled this same city in modern times. The Bible descriptions of the layout of the land and buildings are so accurate; I felt like I was back two thousand years ago walking along the same roads that Jesus and His disciples traveled.

The next morning, our small group gathered together for breakfast at the restaurant in the lobby of our hotel to share a typical Israeli breakfast consisting of fresh juices, eggs, a large variety of soft and hard cheeses, freshly baked breads, olives, jam and butter. We ate to our hearts' delight as we shared the many precious memories we experienced thus far from our trip. We were all excited and looking forward to spending a day at the Western Wall; the Wailing Wall in the old city of Jerusalem. It is considered to be the holiest Jewish site in the world. The western wall is a remnant of the retaining wall built by Herod the Great in the first century B.C. As their only remainder of the sacred destroyed Temple, Jewish people from all over the world gather at this Wall to pray and seek God. It is a common practice for people to write notes to God and place them in between the rocks. I remember my mother telling me when she got back from her trip to Israel, that when she was at the Western Wall, she wrote out prayers to God for my brother and me to have a happy, successful life. I returned the favor by writing out my prayer requests asking God to look over my parents and my brother, and for my marriage to be successful.

There was only one more day left in Jerusalem before we would be heading back home to the States. I chose to leave the group with John that day to visit Yad Vadshem; the Holocaust Museum where Jews and non-Jews alike are remembered after being slaughtered in the death camps in Germany during World War II. The goals of Yad Vadshem are education, research, documentation and commemoration. As I walked into the Museum, I could feel my heart beating so hard, it was hard to catch my breath. Walking from room to room covered with pictures and mementos of Jewish people who were exterminated in the Holocaust, instantly, my thoughts turned to Margaret Gandini and the horrific abuse she endured at the hands of the Nazi soldiers. As I looked at the photographs of the men, woman and children who died because of hatred, I could feel their eyes piercing into my soul. I felt as if they were crying out and saying to me, "Why, why did we have to die before we even got a chance to live?" With tears rolling down my face, I also asked, "Why, what is it in people's hearts that cause them to hate for no reason?" Since it was such a heart wrenching experience, I was only able to stay for a short time. The one positive thing I walked away with was that I have a choice while on this earth to love people and stand against prejudice, injustice and discrimination. I asked, "God give me the courage to stand up for what is right, and stand against what is unjust and cruel."

As soon as I opened my eyes the next morning, the reality set in that my time in Israel was coming to a close. In this short period of time, my heart had become knitted to this land in a way that is hard to describe. Even though America is the land of my birth, Israel is the place my heart found a home. I feel connected to the people, the places, the land, my faith like no other place on earth. It is a country inhabited by people of tremendous strength with an overwhelming desire to thrive and survive. Like Israel, that has become my mantra, "To thrive and survive." When I first started my journey of faith, I struggled with the question, "Can a Jew believe in Jesus?" Walking through this land of the Bible; the land where Jesus taught, performed miracles, and gave His life so that I could have life, I realize, I've come full circle in my Hebrew roots—fully Jewish—fully converted as a disciple of the King of the Jews. I no longer question who He is, and claimed to be. I have evidence for myself. The evidence is a changed life. Yes, I now have the assurance, there are no more doubts; I can be Jewish and a follower of the Jewish Messiah, Y'Shua.

The memories of this land that took my breath away will forever be glued to my soul until I can return once again to this land that I fallen so deeply in love with.

16

Living with Purpose

The plane ride back to the States was long and tiring. While nuzzled in my tiny seat, I looked over at John introspectively, and thought, "Now that our honeymoon is over, it's time to go back home and get to know this man that I've chosen to spend the rest of my life with." During the dating stage, no matter how long that might be, there is no way you can get to know a person until you live with them. I know that doesn't sound very passionate, but it's a reality. Even though I've made my mistakes in matters of the heart, I've still learned a few things. I was past the stage of believing that he was my prince who was going to rescue me from every problem that rears its ugly head. I'd love to believe that life plays out like the movie *Pretty Woman*, where I'm Julia Roberts standing on my terrace while my prince, Richard Gere, comes and rescues me from the stark realities of life. I am not Julia Roberts, and John is not Richard Gere. I certainly don't want to sound like a cynic, being too much of a romantic for that, but at the same time, I didn't want to set myself up with false expectations to get disappointed later on. After pondering these things in my head for a couple of hours, I decided like Scarlet O'Hara in *Gone with the Wind*; "There is always tomorrow to think about these things."

Two years later, in 2003, my mother passed away. A few days before I received the news from my father, she called me. When I answered the phone, I was surprised to hear her voice. It was always my dad who'd make the initial phone call whenever she wanted to speak to me. The conversation was strange in her tone and her hesitancy to get to the point. My mother was not a woman who became flustered when it came to verbal banter. She kept asking how I was and then hesitated as if she wanted to say something but didn't know how to communicate her words. Even though she never got around to telling me why she was calling, I knew that there was something she wasn't telling me. I didn't push the point since she had the tendency to buckle under any confrontation from me in the past. We made small talk for a couple of minutes and then she told me to take care before she hung up the phone. When I hung up, I was bewildered, but let it go since my mother was not a very predictable woman when it came to our one-on-one conversations. That was the last time I ever spoke to my mother. I'd love to tell you that her passing had a profound impact on my emotions, but that was not the case. Even though I'd forgiven her for the trauma she caused me in the past, there was still a part of my heart that had died and closed up as far as she was concerned. Part of the healing process God had done in me where my mother was concerned was revealing to me that I had to give up the dream that my mother and I would ever have the kind of mother-daughter relationship I had longed for as a child. Now, as a grown woman, I've come to understand that her violence towards me was not my fault; it was not because something was wrong with me. No matter what her feelings were toward me, she still had the choice to behave differently.

Judging from that peculiar last phone call, she had something important to say to me that she never was able to express. Yes, I wish she would have had the courage to finally apologize for the horrible things she did to me as a child, but the reality is she didn't. So, although I'll never know why it all happened, I do know that I've moved on and decided to love her anyway. The wounds our parents inflict on us whether it's knowingly or unknowingly take a lifetime to heal. The closure for me is that even though I will never know why, I do know that God as my Father has poured His love into those deep wounds in my heart and removed the poison that tried to destroy me. His perfect love filling up the broken places in my heart is my closure.

Marriage to John has been a growth experience for me. Although he goes to work every day and has never cheated on me, his strong, dominant personality has been a challenge. I've never been the type of woman to take kindly to people's control. In the past, the men in my life have been flexible and easy to get along with; their tendency was to please rather than demand. John likes to have things done his way. He is extremely cautious about every decision he makes. On the positive side, his cautious attitude has helped me to be more responsible. My past tendencies were to make instant decisions before weighing all the options. For example, I had an aged Saturn. It was breaking down way too often and giving me problems. He at the time was driving a Nissan that was also showing her age. I suggested that we get one reliable car instead of having two cars that cost constant money to fix. He said he would consider it. How did it wind up in the end? Two years later, I got a job that required me to drive to Long Island that was two hours travel time round trip. With a little persuading, he finally agreed that we should have one newer, reliable car. So, although I wanted us to purchase the car as soon as I brought it up for discussion,

I had to wait until the time felt right for him. It was worth the wait. When we finally got the car which I picked out, I was tickled pink and extremely grateful. If I hadn't waited, I probably would have not found such a great car that I love. The principal of the story is that all good things come to those who wait. Delaying gratification has helped me to develop patience.

Marriage is not for the faint of heart. Everyone who gets married has certain expectations. In my marriage to John, I've learned to determine the difference between my wants and my needs. When I want things that might not be practical to indulge myself immediately, I surrender it to God and ask Him to decide if I should have it at all. On the other hand, if it is something that is important to me and I deem it worth fighting for, I'm willing to stand up and hold my ground. In essence what I'm saying is that I am careful to pick my battles. I've found that as I change and evolve spiritually, the wants I had years ago have changed. One of my prayers to stay grounded is, "God, let my desires be one with yours, and let my will line up with yours." That is a prayer He has always answered.

John has held me accountable for keeping my word. When I say I'm going to do something he expects me to do it. Accountability is something I've had to learn to commit to God. It says in Matthew 5:37, "Simply let your Yes be Yes and your No be No, anything beyond that comes from the evil one." In essence what Jesus is saying here is to tell the truth. My tendency in the beginning of our relationship was to tell John what I think he should know. If I did something that I did not think was his business, I would tell him only what was convenient to say. God has showed me that answering in that way is not telling the truth—half truths are not the truth. I'm not saying that it was necessary to bare my entire soul to him in every instance; but it is important to God that I answer with correct information. I had to ask myself when I didn't want to tell him something, "Dawn, what is so secretive about what you're doing that you refuse to own up to it? Why didn't I want him to know?" I believe that God was teaching me a lesson about my motives. I've come to understand that whenever God has asked me to do something, He has my best interest at heart, He's not trying to take something from me; rather He is trying to spare me from the pain and destruction that wrongdoing would produce given the chance. After twelve years of marriage, I'm starting to see that John has the same motives as God when he asks me to be honest with him. In conclusion, my marriage to John has had its ups and downs. It is still a work in progress. Thank God we are both on the same page in our commitment to try to make it work.

John does not display his emotions easily but there was one incident that showed me how deeply he cared and loved. After having my cat Max for sixteen years, he got very sick. He had developed a urinary infection which at his age is usually fatal. It broke my heart to see the animal that was like a child to me falling off the bed, not eating, and urinating on himself. John had developed a great affection for Max. Max had also developed a fondness toward John. Many nights, it was John whom he chose to crawl up next to and spend time with. The two of them related well together, and developed a very special bond. Finally, after one week of watching Max deteriorate, John and I brought him to vet. When the veterinarian came out and told us that he was too sick to save, I felt like someone had put a knife through my heart. Of all my pets, Max was my favorite—he was like an angel to me. John and I talked about it, and decided the most merciful thing to do was put him to sleep. When we made that decision, the vet came out and asked us if we would like to be in the room when they gave him the shot.

I knew that I couldn't bear to watch Max being put to sleep. I asked John if he was willing to go in the room and hold Max while they put him down. He said he wanted to be with Max in his last moments. I left the vet's office, went into the car and broke down hysterically. I felt like once again someone that I loved was being taken away from me. When John came out, he got into the car and started to weep. He said, "I loved Max, and I'm going to really miss him." That was a very tender moment that we shared together. It showed me that even though John has a hard outer shell, he still feel things intensely.

Last week, my father called me on his birthday to thank me for the card I sent him. I had mentioned in his birthday card that I'm getting ready to publish my first book. When I picked up the phone, he affirmed me enthusiastically by saying, "Dawn, I'm so excited and proud of you that you have accomplished your goal of writing your book. I can't wait until it's published, so I can read it." He then went on to tell me that he had been giving it some thought and he realized that the things that were done to me as a child were not right. He apologized for the pain that I had suffered. Although he was never the abuser, his apology contributed to my healing. When I hung up the phone, I was blown away. It took 62 years to hear my father tell me that he was proud of me. That meant the world to me. No matter what happened in the past, he is my father and I love him. Even though he was emotionally distant in the past, he also did so many positive things to help me to become the person that I am today. "I thank you dad, for giving me the closure and encouragement. It might have been late in coming, but it still means the world to me." God once again was showing me that in the end, He makes all things right. He is the God of justice.

I cannot finish my story without recognizing my wonderful

LIVING WITH PURPOSE

brother, Bobby Dreyfuss. During the years of my insanity, we might have drifted apart, but now we're closer than ever. He is one of my biggest encouragers. From the start, he has been excited about me telling my story. I love you Bobby! I'm so blessed to have you as my brother.

My intention at this stage of my life is to live with purpose. Instead of just talking about the things I want to accomplish, I'm setting goals and working to achieve them. This is the first time in seven years that I haven't been working full-time. In this year, I've taken off from work so that I could write my memoirs to encourage you, the reader. Writing my story has not been easy for me. I've had to dig deep to pull out the nuggets of wisdom God has given to me. It was very painful for me to go back and visit the dark places in my life. Yet, in order for you to relate to the transformation God has achieved in me, it was necessary to show you the darkness in order for you to see the light. I didn't want to come to the end of my life and realize that I never pursued my dream of telling my life story. It wouldn't be fair to me and it wouldn't be fair to you, my readers. My only hope and prayer is that you have been impacted, and encouraged to see that if God could have taken a life so broken as mine was, He will do the same thing for you no matter what your challenges might be. I beg you to give Him the chance to prove what a truly remarkable God He is. I thank you with all my heart for walking through this journey of wholeness with me. I know from my own experiences that whatever struggles you're facing; if you'll turn to the God who loves you and wants desperately to have a relationship with you, He will come in and answer all your prayers.

If my story has had an impact in your mind or life, this might be your appointed time to take a step forward towards your Creator. He's the one who led me to write my life story—that through the darkness of my past; He may shine His light in your life too. I am grateful to have had the opportunity to share my past sufferings and victories with you, so that through my experiences you can achieve everything you've dreamed of accomplishing. Your Creator is a great God. He uses pain and suffering in our lives to create a perfect vessel for His glory. He first did that with His Son Jesus Christ; let Him also do the same with you. You will never regret it. You will thank Him at the end. He only wishes the best for you, even in the darkest times in your life.

PART IV
Poetry

FIELD OF DREAMS

In the still hours of the night
I like awake, I find myself
thinking of You.

I remember the times I was lost and
confused without direction. I knew
the things I wanted to accomplish.
Yet, the doubts and fears seemed to
take on a life of their own. I am paralyzed
with indecision. The fire of fear has
burnt out all reason.

As I contemplate my next move, suddenly,
I hear a still small voice calling out my name.
My child walk in the midst of the field of dreams.
I say, Lord what is the field of dreams?
All at once, I am standing in a wide open field.
It stretches farther than the eye can see.

I am overwhelmed by the vision in front of me.
A Voice like many rushing waters gets my attention.
Look to the north, the south, the east and the west.
Let my dreams be your dreams. Let my desires become
one with your own. Behold my Bride. From every tribe and
tongue they will come. Suddenly, I observe something that's
too overwhelming for my mind to grasp. In every direction
I see people dressed in their native costume. They are
standing with their hands stretched upwards praising the
Name of Jesus.

They have golden crowns on their heads, and palm leaves in their hands.
They call out in perfect harmony, "holy, holy, holy is the Lord God
Almighty, Who Is and Was and Is to come." They take their crowns
and place them down in front of them. They pay homage to the Name
that is above all Names.

Then, just as the vision was brought into view, it no longer
appears to me. I hear His Voice speak to me with loving authority.
I have shown you my field of dreams. Now, go to every nation,
tongue and tribe and tell them about Me.
The One and Only One Who has all power and authority. When they
Believe, they too will be ushered into the Field of Dreams.

ZION

DAV

CHILD OF PROMISE

In these bitter cold nights,
lying on my bed in a heap of ashes,
the images swirl all around me.
My eyes are hallow, they sink deeper
and deeper within.
My mind is filled with long lost yesterdays,
the tomorrows that are no more.

Coming from the corner of the room,
I encounter a longhaired pearl of a girl.
She is laughing and singing in her flowered
dress and yellow smock. She approaches me.
She does seem to feel the cold and despair
that has become my bitter cup.

She rushes over to me, chuckling loudly.
She cries out, "tip toe, tip toe, little girl
has stubbed her toe.
Mommy's gone so who will know!
Big Daddy in the sky,
He will heal your tattered sigh."

In a flash, my hallow eyes become a sea of tears.
This child of wonder has warmed my lost, lonely heart.
Now, I know Big Daddy in the sky has come to rescue even

DAV   I.   ZION

QUEEN OF HEARTS

She stands proud and tall. Her majestic beauty
is a symbol to all that she is a lady of fancy and grace.
Her splendor comes forth with innocence like finely
woven french lace. When she walks by her smile
invites all who behold her, to follow alongside this rare
specimen, and experience womanhood at its finest.

Who can know or comprehend the heart of a queen?
I have often watched her in the rare moments when she
set aside her jewels of strength. Under the garments of this
paradoxical leader lies the source of her true femininity.
In the moments of her solitude, when she thinks no one is
observing her, I have had the unique privilege of taking vigil.
In these sacred moments, time has become suspended, and
I have taken on a new identity. I am her watchman, her lookout.

In the realm of her domain, this butterfly, this quiet beauty is
transformed. She has emptied herself of all power and authority.
She drops to her knees, lifts her long swanlike neck upwards,
and cries out in a voice that is a whisper. Her eyes start to sparkle
with a glow that is reminiscent of a child opening her first present
on Christmas Day. She has tapped into a source of such joy and
peace, that I too long to join her on this journey.
I hear her speak these words, "God, Father of all that is good
and loving. You alone have given me everything that I will
ever need or want. That gift is Your Son, My Lord,
My Savior, my All and All."

In that moment of time.
I have come to know this queen of hearts.
Her beauty, her charm comes from a higher
place, a place that will never fade with the passing of time.
Without her knowing it, she has given me the greatest gift
I will ever receive. The knowledge that through the One and Only
Living God, I too can become The Queen of Hearts.

ZION

DAV

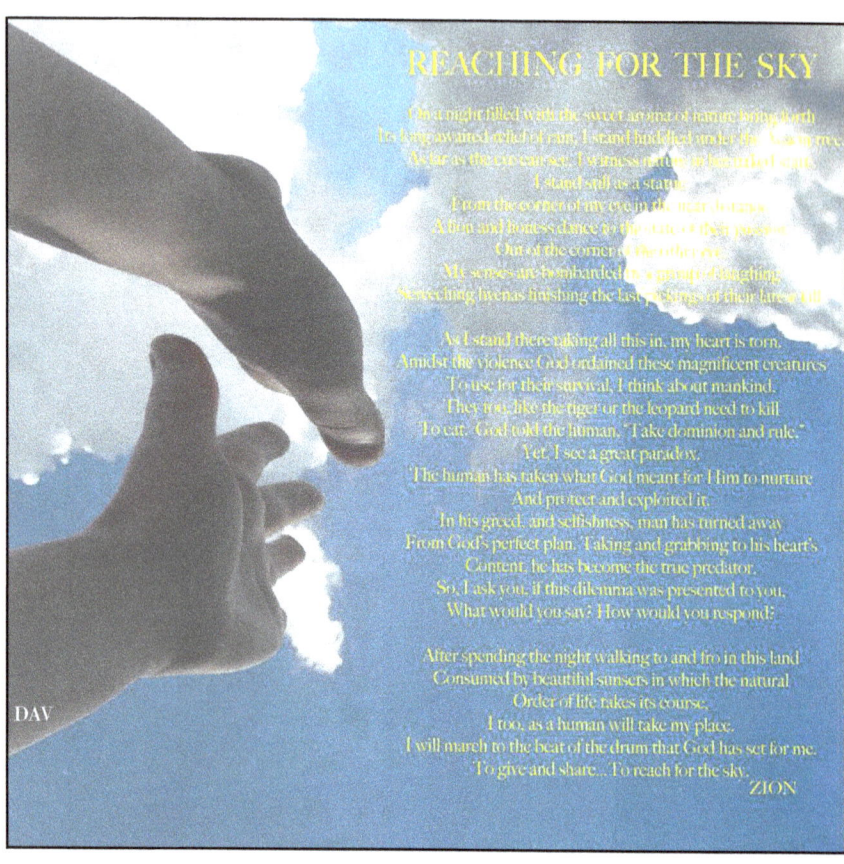

REACHING FOR THE SKY

On a night filled with the sweet aroma of nature bringing forth
Its long awaited relief of rain, I stand huddled under the Acacia tree.
As far as the eye can see, I witness nature in her niche of calm.
I stand still as a statue.
From the corner of my eye in the near distance
A lion and lioness dance to the tune of their passion
Out of the corner of the other eye
My senses are bombarded by a group of laughing
Screeching hyenas finishing the last pickings of their latest kill

As I stand there taking all this in, my heart is torn.
Amidst the violence God ordained these magnificent creatures
To use for their survival, I think about mankind.
They too, like the tiger or the leopard need to kill
To eat. God told the human, "Take dominion and rule,"
Yet, I see a great paradox.
The human has taken what God meant for Him to nurture
And protect and exploited it.
In his greed, and selfishness, man has turned away
From God's perfect plan. Taking and grabbing to his heart's
Content, he has become the true predator.
So, I ask you, if this dilemma was presented to you,
What would you say? How would you respond?

After spending the night walking to and fro in this land
Consumed by beautiful sunsets in which the natural
Order of life takes its course,
I too, as a human will take my place.
I will march to the beat of the drum that God has set for me.
To give and share... To reach for the sky.

ZION

DAV

THE SEA OF DREAMS

There is a place beyond our ordinary reality.
As I walk in this dark, dank city, I lose myself
in the Sea of Dreams.
I am resurrected back to a time,
a place, a memory of You.

It is a new dawn, a new day. The darkness fades
from my consciousness, and bright vivid streams of
Light illuminate Your Face.
You have become my Angel of the moment.
My heart leaps for joy as I reach out and touch You.
I am captivated. We stroll along in fields of
luscious green grass. The smell and sounds add to
my enlightened sensitivity. I am fresh and alive.

Then, just as You blessed me with Your Presence,
You fade out of sight. Nevertheless, I am transformed.
Although I have been brought back to my present reality,
my perspective is new as virgin snow,
sparkling on a chilly winter mourning.
I will praise my Glorious King.
He fills my heart with songs of joy.

ZION

DAV

FREEDOM

Throw down the shackles, break the chains.
Open your mouth wide and shout the victory.
The days of bondage and confinement have ended.
You have arrived into the glorious light.

Look up and you find a heart of joy and peace
that you never known. Your have revoled
in your misery long enough. You have tasted that
bitter cup time and time again. Why delay?
Today is your day to shout a new song.

I will journey through the nations. I will sail the deep
blue seas. I will pour myself out as an offering for
the steadfast Love that I had never known till I
came into Your Kingdom. Every kingdom has a ruler.
You lead Your followers with righteousness and justice.
There is strength and power in Your Hands.

What more can be said of a life such as this?
There is a surety that You offer Your subjects.
I will stand and praise my King and my Leader.
He has made me to walk on the heights.

ZION

DAV

TIME AND TIME AGAIN

Time does not have to be our enemy.
If I decide today to live and love
from moment to moment, I have no need
to befriend the past. I don't have to crawl
back into those painful memories as if they
were a warm blanket. I cannot find my
answers to the dilemma that plagues
my mind and tears at my heart in yesterday.

Instead, I will go on with my life. I'll
concentrate my energies on achieving
the things that I talked about and never
attempted to challenge. By working to
fulfill my dreams and goals, I can look back
at my yesterdays as my best friend.

I want to love myself and others. As a
child of God, I want to fulfill His perfect
plan for my life. I can accomplish this by
deciding that He has given me the precious
gift of my time. Will I use it to glorify Him,
or will I squander it and always wonder why not!

ZION

DAV

UNITY

You are the butcher, the baker, the candlestick maker.
Your skin is black and shinny, mine is white and pale.
You see the world through the eyes of your ancestors.
Your culture and mine are worlds apart.
Yet, we are of one mind and one heart.

There is a cord that binds us together beyond racial lines.
Your Father is my Father. We live and move and have our
being as one Body. Your vision is my vision. Your dreams
for your children is one with mine.

We live together on planet earth, yet, this is not our permanent
Abode. We look forward to a City that is not built with
human hands. We seek a higher, deeper relationship.

Hold my hand and walk with me side by side.
You have become my sister, my brother, my friend.
Let us work together in one accord, for one purpose.
To know and serve Him. To bring a peaceful revolution
to this lost world. We can do it by putting on the
shield of faith. All together as one, becoming a mighty
army marching forward. Raising our banner high,
proclaiming the One and Only Truth.

Arise, awake, the time has come!
Our Savior, our Deliver declares...
His invitation is clear. Come One, Come All.
Rejoice, the victory has been won!
He is calling...You know Him.
His Name is the King of Kings and Lord of Lords.

ZION

DAV

LION KING

Who is the lion in the Tribe of Judah?
In the black thicket of the jungle night,
As the wind howls, and all the creatures
Violently dance out their drama,
A bright radiant Light appears on the scene.

Within a heartbeat, a sound like many rushing waters
Picks up momentum. All the nightlife come to a stand still.
Behold! The King takes center stage.
All eyes pop open, mouths zipper up.
Creation waits for their cue.

Suddenly a Voice cries out.
Bring me the Lamb and the Dove.
Without hesitation out of nowhere,
They appear side by side.
The King surrounds them.
He questions the creatures of the night.
Who is like unto These?

All faces everywhere shine bright.
Every tongue responds simultaneously.
Let homage be paid to Them in full.
For They alone have created harmony
NOW and FOREVER!
ZION

THE FIRE WITHIN

Disjointed, alone and out of pocket.
I wander around another day, viewing the
world from a place of discord. My heart
yearns to return to the warm candle that
burns so bright. Whosoever experiences
It's Presence, could not help coming away
transformed and parched for a drink of Living Water.

As I watch this world grow colder, grabbing tighter
for the things that hold only momentary pleasure,
I am brought to the stark reality of knowing the
answer to the futile battle. The Voice of Reason
within my heart offers a solution. "Strive not to
wear yourself out struggling to acquire those things
that eventually rot and decay with time. Instead choose
the higher path that leads to peace, joy and great expectancy.
Pursue the things that are above, not the empty trivialities
which leave people destitute and crying out for more."

Now that the Voice of Authority settled the conflict in my heart,
I am intact, solid and undivided. The fire that burns within
has been resurrected. I am no longer alone. I am once again
with the One and Only Lover of my soul.

ZION

DAV

WARFARE

Showers spill
Drop...by...drop.
All God's children march
One...by...one.
Guns are slaughtering
Bullet...by...bullet.

Pop goes the weasel.
Deadly still.
Breathe...
It just slowly fizzles out.

ZION

A BEACON OF LIGHT

Who are our heroes?
Who are our stars?
Is it the raven haired beauty on the cover
of the latest fashion magazine?
Or maybe it's the NBA's latest draft pick
that will receive a $50 million dollar contract?
Or maybe it's the real estate magnate with a penthouse
in New York, and a summer home in Spain?
I ask you, what are the ingredients that makes one a champion?

To me it's quite simple.
It's the fire fighter who knows the building is going down
after the bomb hit, and goes back in to rescue the
old woman on the 46th floor in a wheel chair.
It's the iron fitter and steel worker who give up
their paychecks to spend days sifting through a mountain heap
of refuge and death to rescue one human being.

Yes, it's you and me, who'll stay up all night with a hurting friend.
It's you and me, in the face of danger that will help a stranger.
It's you and me who'll gave the homeless with AIDS a hot meal.
I ask you, what is true spirituality?
What is true love for our fellow man?
In the face of God, where do you stand?
Are you a beacon of light?

ZION

DAV

MY DAD

Here is a man so proud and true.
Your heart is pure gold through and through,
Whenever there is a care, or problem too,
You take the time in spite of all you do.

I want to proclaim on this special day,
It's your words of instruction
And wisdom to me,
Which have so much to say

You're a father of faithfulness
And much love too,
I thank God so much for
Giving me you.

VALENTINE'S DAY LOVE

On this special Day my love,
I proclaim to you my words
Of happiness and joy my gentle dove.
As I awake and begin every day,
It's your sweet face that guides
My heart and directs my way.

When the storms of life come
In like a flood, your glorious face
And eyes of magic is what
I embrace.
To you alone I give my all,
My song, my tears, my
life, that's my true call.

So, it is only fitting that
On this day, I remind you
Again my love…
You are my bliss, my delight
And my only true light.
Happy Valentine's Day
To my one and only.

ZION

THE COLORS OF LOVE

Like an artist that splatters paint on a canvas,
So is your gentle hand that smears yellow
Sunlight in circles around my heart.
In the blackness of the night my eyes
Search for the sparkle in your iridescent smile.
As I write your portrait in the sky,
It is you my love, like a kaleidoscope of
Brilliant colors that lights my path.
No matter what life brings,
Your love is the warm candle
That guides my way.
You are the Valentine I love

Whispers in the Night

As the sun fades down beneath the rocky emerald shore,
The sweet perfume of our music beckons my heart,
Oh sweet bird of paradise, your voice restrains me,
You know the way that I go. The darkness reveals
The song that light could not tell.

Goodbye is the strains and pains that hide in the daylight.
The struggle to know and do it all.
Now, the hands that reach for the moon comes home.

Time for starry skies and midnight moonbeams.

We'll listen to the angels play their songs.
In our dreams, hand in hand,
Together we breathe in whispers of the night
Zion

Debra Vatalaro

TREE OF LIFE

Love and loss are the passions that grind and tremble

In the crevices of the night.
As I sit above you, my heart is searching... it's groaning

Your pain is calling to me.
Oh sweet child of wonder
The bells are ringing; they are singing your name.

Your song is sweet to me...like the buds
Pregnant with life
Come to me now. I will feed on your youth.
You will feed on my love that
Has smoldered the fires of loss.

Let's climb the ladder.
Together we will ride the shooting stars.
We will look down upon the ugly faces
Of hate and betrayal,
Only to abandon ourselves into the branches
Of the Tree of Life.

ZION

Debra Vatalaro

To My Daughter

When you were born,
you were my pride and joy.
Now you have left childhood things aside
And become a strong, beautiful woman.

I want you to know that although we are miles apart,
You are still the apple of my eye. You have grown
And matured into a glorious eaglet that soars majestically.
Your life is full of vision and promise.

Through many trials and struggles you have come
Forth as pure gold. Your husband rises and calls you
Blessed above all women. You have clothed yourself
With dignity and strength. The future is now something
You can look forward to., and be excited about.

On this special day, I want you to know how proud
You have made me. My dear, I await the day that I
Can see you face to face. My dear daughter
I love you and always will.

ZION

Debra Vatalaro

OUR SECRET PLACE

My love comes quickly.
This fire inside can
Only be fulfilled through
Looking into Your Eyes.

I desire to meet
In our secret place.
In this secluded spot, time is suspended,
And we are together in our private oasis.
Here, I can speak words of love to you.
We can dance together with the
Wind and the rain as our only interference.

The time has come.
I feel you by my side.
Into your arms I fall.
You carry me away.
My joy is complete.
You have fulfilled the emptiness
Within my soul. I have come alive.
Now, I never have to be alone again.

ZION

*Debra Vatalaro

YOUR LOVING EYES

When the night breaks the silence
That the day could not hold,
Your Light streams through walls of glass.
It breaks up the dead carcass that
Lingers within my wretched heart.

I grapple for strength.
Arms chasing, feet chasing,
Going around in circles,
Searching for that nod of approval
That lies within your Loving Eyes.

Here alone in that place inside
The crease of Your Smile –
The Splendor, the resurrection,
Freedom from tyranny.
The fusion of heart and spirit.
     Zion

ILLUSIONS

In a world of make believe
Where spiders dance on dead eyes
and sea urchins weave their magic
On golden sand castles,
I catch a glimpse of Your oceanic Eyes.

You shine brighter than the sun.
Draw me closer for a taste of your warmth.
The waves are breaking, the fire is burning.
I am cold and empty. I shiver beneath
The lopsided moon that holds Your
Love like an anchor. Draw me into
The grip, the tight clench that hides
My hungry heart.

Where were You when I was dancing,
Prancing, running in circles, chasing my
Fantasies beneath my feet, casting
My nets upon a bottomless ocean.

As I turn aside from my wantonness,
I reach up, up, up, and I find what
I wanted all along. There you are,
Waiting, calling, singing the song,
The melody. I embrace Your Love,
I look into Your Oceanic Eyes,
No longer casting my nets upon
My bottomless sea.

Debra Vatalaro ZION

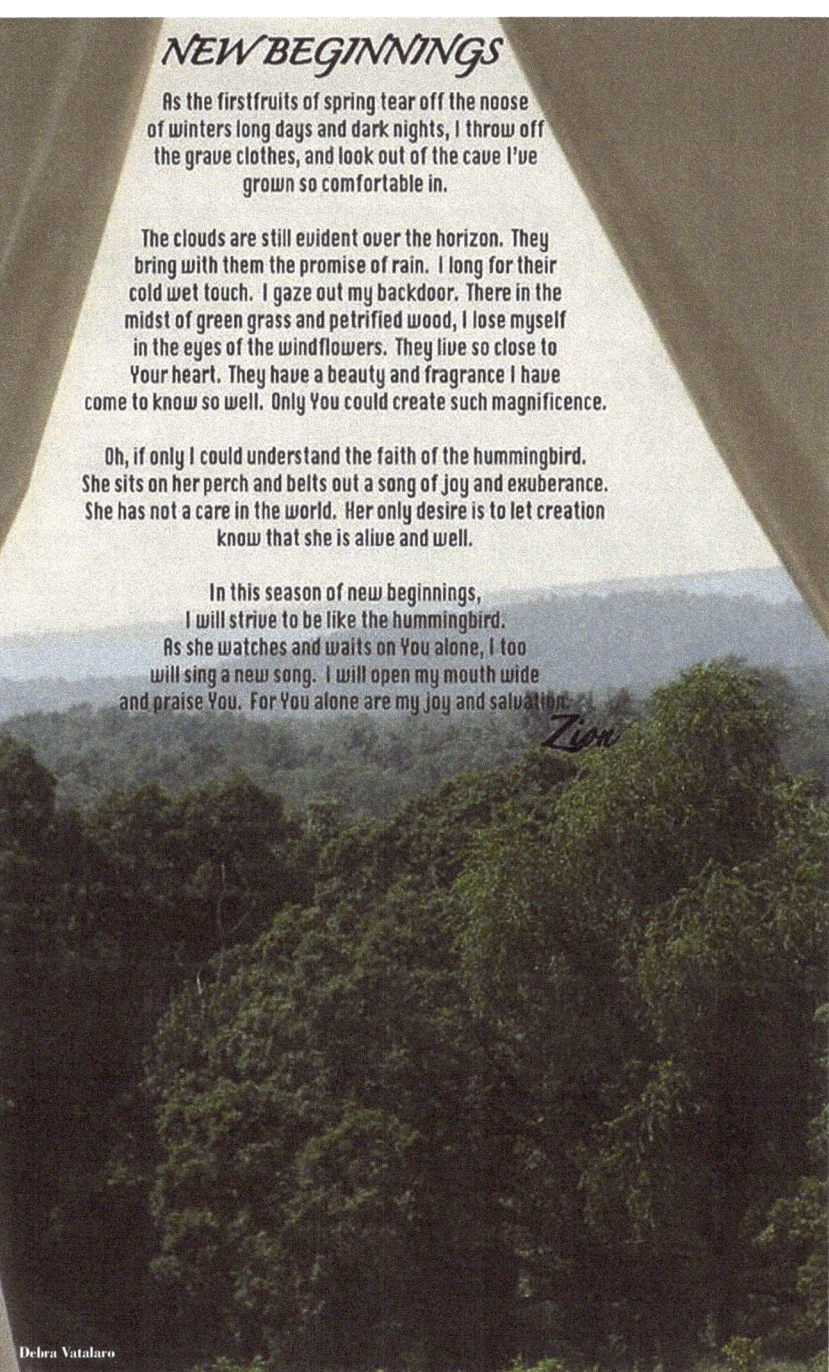

NEW BEGINNINGS

As the firstfruits of spring tear off the noose
of winters long days and dark nights, I throw off
the grave clothes, and look out of the cave I've
grown so comfortable in.

The clouds are still evident over the horizon. They
bring with them the promise of rain. I long for their
cold wet touch. I gaze out my backdoor. There in the
midst of green grass and petrified wood, I lose myself
in the eyes of the windflowers. They live so close to
Your heart. They have a beauty and fragrance I have
come to know so well. Only You could create such magnificence.

Oh, if only I could understand the faith of the hummingbird.
She sits on her perch and belts out a song of joy and exuberance.
She has not a care in the world. Her only desire is to let creation
know that she is alive and well.

In this season of new beginnings,
I will strive to be like the hummingbird.
As she watches and waits on You alone, I too
will sing a new song. I will open my mouth wide
and praise You. For You alone are my joy and salvation.

Zion

Debra Vatalaro

LIVING STONES

As this long lifeless winter steps aside, I peek out of my lonely stony shell that has entrenched my hungry heart. Life a martyr that fought her empty 'cause, I awaken spontaneously to a new reality.

I walk alongside a winding path. I see the first hint of daisies and honeysuckles peeking out of their perfumed petals. The wind blows a wisp of hair in my eyes. I inhale the breeze, and smell the sweet promise of the first spring rain. The earth is coming alive with laughter, hope, and the promise of good days ahead.

As I reflect on all the fears and tears, I have held so close to my heart, I realize they also had their purpose in this life God gives us. Just as the flowers grow in their season of time, there is a season for us to grow as well.

We should not be consumed with living and getting happiness just for ourselves. How much we would miss, if, that was our only mission. There is so much more to our pilgrimage than that. We have the privilege of giving ourselves to one another, unselfishly, that makes the coming out of the shell worthwhile.

        ZION

Debra Vatalaro

THE FUSION OF LOVE

On a bright September day,
Where there were no clouds, nor rain, nor haze,
in a quiet and discreet way
you made an entrance, a glance, a look, a gaze.

From the opposite ends of the earth you came.
So different, so unique, yet we are the same.
Like birds that fly and soar as one,
Compared to you my love, there is none.

What was God thinking when He brought you to me?
What was it He wanted you and me to see?
A dream, a phase, a waltz in the sand;
A life together walking hand in hand.

As I paint your portrait in the sky,
seeing you in mind's eye,
Can this tiger truly be tamed?
She is the one that you have named.

My life, my love is for you to keep,
a river, a valley, a mountain not too deep.
You alone have shown me a brand new day,
And together as one we'll make our way.
                                    Zion

Debra Vatalaro

Here's wishing that the joy
that this magical Season holds
Brim your heart with overwhelming
happiness, goodness and generosity

Letting all the blessings from above
Abound and overflow in great measure.

Have a Blessed Christmas and
Prosperous New Year!

To My Mother

WHAT MY MOM IS

You are the jewel in my life,
Your love is wider than the ocean blue,
Your kindness is there no matter what I do.
Your wisdom guides and leads my way,
Your smile is the light that brightens my day.
Your heart is pure gold, through and through.
You gave the gift of life to me,
You gave me eyes that I could see
All the wonderful things you mean to me.

ZION

HAPPY MOTHER'S DAY TO MY MOM THE LIONESS

Debra Vatalaro

Prayer

Before I put down my pen, I want to give you an opportunity to invite the Lord Jesus Christ into your life. In doing this, I want to emphasize that by praying this you are not joining a religion. You are asking the God who created you to come and live in you and have a deep relationship with you. He loves you and is waiting for you to come to Him.

"Behold, I stand at the door and knock. If any man (or woman) hears my voice and opens the door, I will come in to him and dine with him, and he with Me." Revelation 3:20.

Dear Father God, I've tried to live life on my own terms, and have fallen short. Lord, I am a sinner. There is no other God who can forgive my sins except Your Son Jesus Christ. You have sent Him on this earth to save me by sacrificing Himself for me. He willingly went to the cross and shed His precious blood as the atonement for my sins, past, present and future. Lord Jesus, I open the door of my heart and invite you to come in and live in my heart forever. I want you to be the Lord of my life; body, mind and spirit. Today, I surrender everything in my life to you, trusting that you will give me eternal life and peace. I pray that You fill me with the Holy Spirit who is going to guide, lead, teach and remind me about you. I want to hear Your voice and receive direction for my life. Thank you for hearing my prayer and giving me the chance to have a relationship with You. I receive it now, in Jesus Name. Amen!

Contact Page

If you would like to write me with your comments and questions, I would love to hear from you. Please share with me how God has encouraged you or challenged you while reading my book.

I am open to speak and share my story of deliverance wherever I am invited.

You can reach me by E-mail at: dawn.dreyfuss777@gmail.com

May God bless you all with His richest blessings.

www.ingramcontent.com/pod-product-compliance
Lightning Source LLC
Chambersburg PA
CBHW050800160426
43192CB00010B/1590